Inventors Who Changed the World

Philo T. Farnsworth

Visionary Inventor of Television

Tim O'Shei

MyReportLinks.com Books

an imprint of

Enslow Publishers, Inc.

Box 398, 40 Industrial Road
Berkeley Heights, NJ 07922
USA

To Buffalo State College's International Center for Studies in Creativity, the place where future Farnsworth's are nurtured.

MyReportLinks.com Books, an imprint of Enslow Publishers, Inc. MyReportLinks® is a registered trademark of Enslow Publishers, Inc.

Library of Congress Cataloging-in-Publication Data

O'Shei, Tim.
  Philo T. Farnsworth : visionary inventor of television / Tim O'Shei.
      p. cm. — (Inventors who changed the world)
  Includes bibliographical references and index.
  ISBN-13: 978-1-59845-075-0 (hardcover)
  ISBN-10: 1-59845-075-1 (hardcover)
  1. Farnsworth, Philo Taylor, 1906-1971—Juvenile literature. 2. Television—Biography—Juvenile literature. 3. Inventors—United States—Biography—Juvenile literature. 4. Electric engineers—United States—Biography—Juvenile literature. 5. Television—History—Juvenile literature. I. Title.
  TK6635.F3O84 2008
  621.3880092—dc22
  [B]

                                    2007005461

Printed in the United States of America

10 9 8 7 6 5 4 3 2 1

To Our Readers:
Through the purchase of this book, you and your library gain access to the Report Links that specifically back up this book.

The Publisher will provide access to the Report Links that back up this book and will keep these Report Links up to date on **www.myreportlinks.com** for five years from the book's first publication date.

We have done our best to make sure all Internet addresses in this book were active and appropriate when we went to press. However, the author and the Publisher have no control over, and assume no liability for, the material available on those Internet sites or on other Web sites they may link to.

The usage of the MyReportLinks.com Books Web site is subject to the terms and conditions stated on the Usage Policy Statement on **www.myreportlinks.com**.

A password may be required to access the Report Links that back up this book. The password is found on the bottom of page 4 of this book.

Any comments or suggestions can be sent by e-mail to comments@myreportlinks.com or to the address on the back cover.

♻ Enslow Publishers, Inc. is committed to printing our books on recycled paper. The paper in every book contains between 10% to 30% post-consumer waste (PCW). The cover board on the outside of each book contains 100% PCW. Our goal is to do our part to help young people and the environment too!

Photo Credits: Academy of Television Arts & Sciences, p. 34; American Museum of Natural History/The Hebrew University/Skirball, p. 92; AP/Wide World Photos, pp. 10, 46, 54–55, 84, 94–95; Bairdtelevision.com, p. 44; Boston University Office of University Relations, p. 74; Cable News Network LP, LLLP, p. 88; CondéNet Inc., p. 68; Courtesy of MagazineArt.org, p. 27; David Sarnoff Collection, p. 50; Early Television Foundation and Museum, p. 76; Farnsworth Archives, pp. 5, 18–19, 21, 28, 42, 82–83; Federal Communications Commission, p. 89; Finca Blanca Media, LLC, p. 79; IEEE, p. 43; Kinema, pp. 63, 70; Library of Congress, p. 81; Mall-USA, Inc., p. 90; Manuscripts Division, University of Utah Libraries, pp. 1 (receiver), 30–31, 36–37, 48, 110; Massachusetts Institute of Technology, p. 67; *Modern Mechanix*, p. 61; MyReportLinks.com Books, p. 4; National Inventors Hall of Fame Foundation, Inc., p. 116; National Museum of Education, p. 114; NPR, p. 107; Oak Tree Press, p. 33; Paul Schatzkin, pp. 11, 59; PBS/WGBH, p. 52; Photos.com, p. 106; sfmuseum.org, p. 65; Shutterstock.com, pp. 8–9, 16–17, 24–25, 40–41, 72–73, 86–87, 102, 104–105, 112; Tarlton Law Library/The University of Texas School of Law, p. 100; The Museum of Broadcast Communications, p. 49; The New York Times Company, p. 109; Time, Inc., p. 13; University Libraries, University of Maryland, p. 75; Utah Historical Society, p. 1 (portrait); WGBH Educational Foundation, p. 98.

Cover Photos: Manuscripts Division, University of Utah Libraries (receiver); Utah Historical Society (portrait).

CONTENTS

MyReportLinks.com Books
Great Books, Great Links, Great for Research!

The Internet sites featured in this book can save you hours of research time. These Internet sites—we call them **"Report Links"**—are constantly changing, but we keep them up to date on our Web site.

When you see this "Approved Web Site" logo, you will know that we are directing you to a great Internet site that will help you with your research.

Give it a try! Type http://www.myreportlinks.com into your browser, click on the series title and enter the password, then click on the book title, and scroll down to the Report Links listed for this book.

The Report Links will bring you to great source documents, photographs, and illustrations. MyReportLinks.com Books save you time, feature Report Links that are kept up to date, and make report writing easier than ever! A complete listing of the Report Links can be found on pages 118–119 at the back of the book.

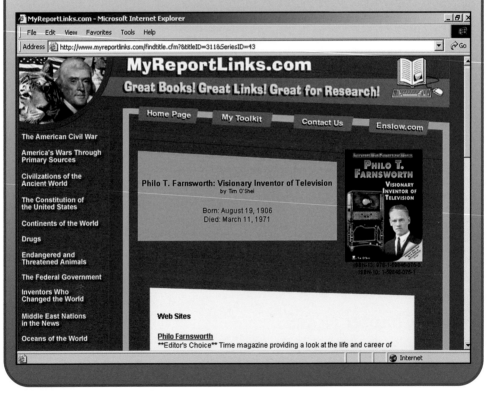

Please see "To Our Readers" on the copyright page for important information about this book, the MyReportLinks.com Web site, and the Report Links that back up this book.

Please enter PTF1677 if asked for a password.

Television is a gift of God, and God will hold those who utilize his divine instrument accountable to him.

—Philo T. Farnsworth

IMPORTANT DATES

1906 —Philo Taylor Farnsworth is born in the small town of Indian Creek, Utah, on August 19.

1918 —In the spring, the Farnsworth family moves to their uncle's farm in Rigby, Idaho.

1922 —The Farnsworths move to Provo, Utah. Philo stays behind, working as a railroad electrician, to save money for college.

1923 —Philo joins his family in Utah and enrolls as a "special student" at Brigham Young University so he can finish his high school courses. At BYU, he studies math and science, and he works in the glass lab.

1924 —When Lewis Farnsworth (father) dies from pneumonia, Philo drops out of college to support his family.

—Philo Farnsworth briefly attends the U.S. Naval Academy in Annapolis, Maryland. He then returns to Utah, shortening his name to "Phil."

1926 —Farnsworth begins working with George Everson and Leslie Gorrell, who invest in his idea of producing an electric television. The three partners open an office in Los Angeles, California, to be near the resources of the California Institute of Technology and the Hollywood film industry.

—Farnsworth marries Elma "Pem" Gardner in May, and they move to Los Angeles. In September, Phil and Pem Farnsworth move to San Francisco, where bankers agreed to support his work.

1927 —*September 7:* Farnsworth successfully creates the first image by an electric television: he transmits a single line onto a small screen in his laboratory.

1928 —Farnsworth improves his television, creating clearer images. He shows off his work at a press conference on September 1.

—Farnsworth's laboratory burns to the ground in October and is rebuilt. In December, the company reopens under the name Television Laboratories.

1929 —*September:* Phil and Pem Farnsworth welcome their first son Philo, Jr.

—*October 29:* The stock market crashes, starting the Great Depression and leaving Television Laboratories needing money.

1930 —Working for RCA, Vladimir Zworykin spies on Farnsworth's television developments. In August, the U.S. government grants Farnsworth patents for his television scanning and receiving systems.

1931 —*May:* Farnsworth Laboratories makes a deal with radio manufacturer Philco, to compete with RCA.

—*July:* The Farnsworths move to Philadelphia, the new location of Farnsworth Laboratories.

1932 —Phil and Pem Farnsworth face tragedy: they lose almost all of their money when their bank closes, and their infant son Kenny dies from a throat infection.

1933 —Farnsworth splits from Philco to continue his work on the television.

1935 —*July:* The U.S. Patent Office concludes that Farnsworth, not RCA, invented television.

1936 —While traveling in Europe, Farnsworth helps John Logie Baird set up an electronic television system, which a fire later destroys.

1938 —The Farnsworths purchase a farm in Fryeburg, Maine.

1939 —*March:* The Farnsworth Television & Radio Corporation becomes a public company, raising $3 million from investors.

—*April:* David Sarnoff of RCA claims credit for starting the era of television. Black-and-white sets are sold to the public for the first time, with NBC airing the television shows.

—Edwin Nicholas takes charge of the Farnsworth company, leading to a licensing deal between RCA and Farnsworth. Farnsworth receives $1 million plus royalties.

1941 —*December 7:* Japan attacks Pearl Harbor. Materials that would have made televisions are now made into war supplies, and nearly all television broadcasting stops.

1947 —A fire destroys the Farnsworths' Maine home and laboratory, worth many thousands of dollars. The family moves to Boston for the winter.

1948 —After discussions with Einstein, Farnsworth begins planning a fusion machine that would produce cheap and safe energy.

1960 —*October:* Farnsworth tests his first fusion machine, called the Fusor, and successfully produces a miniature star.

1971 —Philo Farnsworth dies at age sixty-four on March 11 due to pneumonia.

"THERE YOU HAVE ELECTRONIC TELEVISION"

As Philo Farnsworth drove to work one foggy fall morning in 1927, he hoped the day was going to grow bright. Farnsworth and his small staff had been working for many months at perfecting a dream. On this morning, he knew they were very, very close to making it a reality.

What was Farnsworth's dream? He wanted to use a camera to electronically break apart a picture, shoot it through the air, and show it on a screen. He wanted to mix movies and radio to create a new technology: electronic television.

When Farnsworth told people about his project, they often looked puzzled. "Tele-*what?*" they would ask. If he tried to explain that he was working on a way to

CHAPTER 1

transmit radio waves that would form a picture, people usually became even more confused. They did not get it, but Farnsworth did. He had first dreamed up the idea seven years earlier, when he was only fourteen years old. Now he was twenty-one on this misty morning of September 7, 1927, in San Francisco, California, and he was closer than ever to making his vision a reality.

➔ RADIO RULES THE WORLD

Life in 1920s America was far different from what it is today. People got their news by listening to the radio or reading the newspaper. The lightbulb was fairly new. Many adults had likely spent their childhood growing up without electricity in their homes. Families would not have computers for more than a half century in the future. Video games, DVD players, and MP3 players did not exist.

Known as the forgotten father of television, Philo Farnsworth was just a teenager when he first envisioned the idea of electronic television.

Young people entertained themselves by playing outdoor games, reading, or going to short black-and-white silent movies. Or, of course, by listening to the radio. It would not be long before the invention of television would change all of that. It would become people's number one source of news and entertainment.

While other inventors were working on television, their approach was different from Farnsworth's. They were trying to develop *mechanical* television, by which a spinning disk captured bits of light and transmitted these beams onto a screen. Farnsworth knew this would never work well. In his mind, the best way

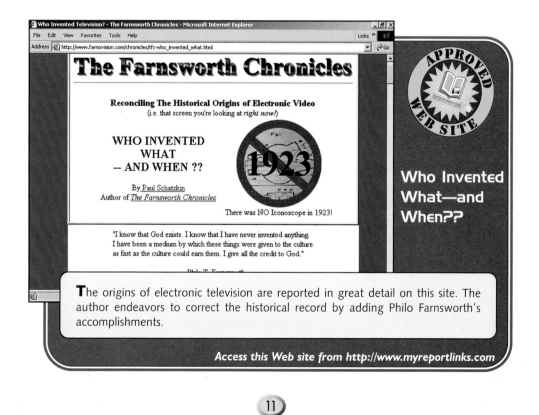

The origins of electronic television are reported in great detail on this site. The author endeavors to correct the historical record by adding Philo Farnsworth's accomplishments.

Access this Web site from http://www.myreportlinks.com

to capture and reproduce an image was to break it into countless electrons and transmit them through the air to a receiver that would piece the image back together. This was based on the principles of electricity and magnetism. No moving parts were necessary. Farnsworth was correct: *Electronic* television was indeed better. But it would take years of struggle before the world found out he was right.

The Vision Works!

On that September morning in 1927, Farnsworth's goal was simple: He wanted to point a camera at a glass slide with a straight line painted across it and make it appear on a screen in another room. But accomplishing that goal was extremely complicated.

During the past several months, Farnsworth had tried eleven experiments with electronic television. They failed each time. Like any good inventor, Farnsworth learned from his failures. Every time an experiment did not work, Farnsworth tried to figure out why and then fix the problem.

So far, Farnsworth had done that over and over. He was hoping the twelfth experiment would finally be the one that made history. Farnsworth's employees joined him in the lab that morning. Those present included his wife,

Elma G. "Pem" Farnsworth, her brother Cliff Gardner, and engineers Carl Christensen and Bob Humphries.

They used a partition to split the room into two parts. On one side was the simple camera, called the Image Dissector. A receiving tube was on the other side. Gardner was by the Image Dissector. He held in his hand a glass slide with a straight line painted across it. Phil and Pem Farnsworth and the engineers stood near the receiver.

TIME 100: Philo Farnsworth - Microsoft Internet Explorer

File   Edit   View   Favorites   Tools   Help   Links »

Address http://www.time.com/time/time100/scientist/profile/farnsworth.html   Go

THE TIME 100   1901   2000   The Most Important People of the Century

LEADERS & REVOLUTIONARIES | ARTISTS & ENTERTAINERS | BUILDERS & TITANS | SCIENTISTS & THINKERS | HEROES & ICONS

CORBIS

Inventor Philo T. Farnsworth with his invention, the first electronic television, in Sept. 10, 1928 in San Francisco

■ SCIENTISTS & THINKERS
Philo Farnsworth

PERSON OF THE CENTURY

Albert Einstein
He was unfathomably profound — the genius among geniuses who discovered, merely by thinking about it, that the universe was not as it seemed. More >>

Runner-Up: F.D.R.
Runner-Up: Gandhi

>> Try 4 issues of TIME magazine Risk-Free!

ADVERTISEMENT

UNLIMITED A
MILLI
OF SO

APPROVED WEB SITE

Considered one of the key visionary minds of the twentieth century, Philo T. Farnsworth began his life on a farm in Utah. Find out how he conceived the idea of electronic television when you visit this **Philo Farnsworth** Web page.

EDITOR'S CHOICE

"Put in the slide, Cliff," Farnsworth directed.[1] Cliff Gardner slipped the slide between the Image Dissector and a bright lamp.

In the other room, Farnsworth and the small crowd watched the screen. It flickered. After a few moments, a small line appeared. At first, the image was blurry. Farnsworth adjusted the focus, and the line became clear.

Farnsworth shouted to Cliff Gardner to turn the slide. When he did, the line moved as well. "That's it, folks!" Farnsworth said. "We've done it! There you have electronic television."[2]

⇒No Doubt About It

"If I wasn't seeing it with my own two eyes, I wouldn't believe it," Christensen said. Humphries simply smiled. Just then, Everson arrived at the lab. After witnessing the first-ever television image, he patted Farnsworth on the back. "There's no doubt about it Phil," he said. "My faith in you all these months has been justified."[3]

Farnsworth and Everson sent a telegraph to another partner, Leslie Gorrell, who was in Los Angeles. The message was simple: "The damned thing works!"[4]

This was only the beginning. At this moment, television was nothing more than a single line on a small screen in a San Francisco laboratory. It would take years to transform television into a technology that delivered moving pictures with sound into millions of homes.

Still, this breakthrough was a start. Until today, no one had been able to electronically transmit an image that could move on a screen. Few people knew about it, but this was big news indeed.

How the Dream Began

CHAPTER

2

Philo Farnsworth helped create a world in which people are entertained by staring at a box with moving pictures and sound. But the world he was born into was much different.

Philo Taylor Farnsworth was born on August 19, 1906, in a tiny Utah town called Indian Creek. He was the oldest child of Lewis and Serena Farnsworth, who would later add two boys and two girls to their family. The Farnsworths were farmers and they moved often, always looking for fertile land. They were poor and led simple lives. Their fanciest possession was a hand-cranked record player called a gramophone.

➔ Moving to Idaho

In the spring of 1918, the Farnsworths packed their belongings into three wagons and moved

north to the state of Idaho. Lewis Farnsworth knew that Idaho had plenty of cheap land that was good for growing crops. But the Farnsworths did not have enough money right away to buy their own farm. Instead, they planned to move in with their uncle, Albert Farnsworth, who owned a farm in Rigby, Idaho. Their plan was to stay there until they could afford land.

The trip took several weeks. When the family finally reached Uncle Albert's property, Philo grew excited. He saw wires hanging between the buildings. That meant Uncle Albert's farm had electricity!

Uncle Albert's farm was on 240 acres of land surrounded by mountains and forests and located near the Snake River. The farm was about the size of 180 football fields. Potatoes and sugar beets were the main crops. Twelve-year-old Philo was old enough to do chores around the house and farm. He did them, but he hated chores. Farming

Philo T. Farnsworth was born in this cabin in Indian Creek, Utah. His family led a simple farming life. Their house bore no comforts, including electricity.

was not for him. Philo was much more interested in science and inventions. Philo was especially intrigued by an electric generator that Uncle Albert kept in a shed. That generator powered everything from the barn lights to the the sewing machine. Whenever the generator broke down, Philo watched the local repairman, William Tall, tinker with it. Philo was a good observer. Soon he understood better than anyone else how the generator worked.

⊜ Good Work

One day, when the generator seemed broken beyond repair, Philo saw the problem differently. He could tell the parts were not broken. They were clogged with grease and simply needed a good cleaning. Philo begged Uncle Albert to let him take a shot at fixing the generator. Uncle Albert let him do it. Piece by piece, Philo took the generator apart. He carefully cleaned the grease and dirt from each part, then reassembled the generator. Soon it hummed back to life. Uncle Albert patted Philo on the shoulder. Lewis Farnsworth wrapped his arms around his boy and said, "Good work, son."[1]

Lewis encouraged his son to keep working on electronics, and that is just what Philo did. He even found ways to use electricity to make his chores pass faster. One of the chores he wanted to

Philo's father, Lewis Farnsworth.

avoid was running the family's hand-operated machine for washing clothes. Philo found a broken motor, fixed it, and connected it to the washer. Philo found that the motor could do his job of turning the insides of the washer. The motor could wash the clothes for him. Philo had replaced himself with an electric washing machine—which was just fine by him!

⇒A Scientific Dreamer

Philo set his alarm for four o'clock every morning. He spent the first hour of each day reading about science. Uncle Albert's attic was stacked with science magazines like *Popular Science* and *Science and Invention,* along with Sears, Roebuck & Company catalogs that featured all the latest electrical contraptions. This was part of Philo's self-education in electronics. He also saved his money to buy an encyclopedia and enrolled in the National Radio Institute to become a "radiotrician." In that job he could build radios, transmitters, and work on wiring other types of electronics.

Philo spent a lot of time dreaming up inventions. Sometimes he got caught dreaming when he needed to be focused on something else. One day, Philo was sitting atop a plow pulled by three horses. He was busy thinking about an invention idea and was holding only two of the three pairs of reins. His father was standing far across the field and saw this. Lewis Farnsworth's heart started racing. Those reins were the only way to control the horses. He knew that if the third horse got startled it could rampage away, throwing Philo off the top of the plow and into the rotating blades.

Quickly but quietly, trying not to startle the horse, Lewis Farnsworth walked toward the plow. As he neared Philo, Lewis reminded his son to grab the reins. Philo, unconcerned by the danger, yelled, "Papa, papa, I've got it!"[2]

Young Philo began explaining that he had an idea for winning a science magazine contest. But Lewis, still nervous, did not want to hear it and scolded Philo for his carelessness and risk of death he put himself in. "Philo," he said, "you could have been killed!"[3]

⇒ Prize Worthy?

Later that night, Lewis asked Philo about the idea. Philo explained that *Science and Invention* magazine was holding a contest. The prize for the best invention was twenty-five dollars, which would have been worth about $475 in 2007. Philo had an idea that would prevent automobiles from being easily stolen. Back then, cars used very basic keys. It was easy to take a straight piece of metal, stick it in the ignition to start a car, and drive away. Philo wanted to develop a magnetic ignition

The plow that young Philo was working when he thought up the idea for television was a harrow, like the one shown here.

switch. Both the key and the ignition would be magnetized, so one had to attract the other in order for the car to start.

Philo sent a detailed description of his idea to *Science and Invention*. It won! Philo Farnsworth, just a young teenager, had envisioned an idea that beat others from across the county.

This was just the start. Philo had much bigger and better ideas. One of them dominated his mind: He had visions of a contraption that could make pictures fly through the air.[4] Soon enough, he would act on it.

Visions of Television

Philo attended Rigby High School, in Idaho, and breezed through the science and math classes intended for students his age. He talked his way into a chemistry class for older students. The teacher, Mr. Justin Tolman, was impressed with Philo's ability to understand complex information. Sometimes, in fact, Philo taught classes himself.

When Philo was fourteen, he felt ready to describe his idea that would add pictures to radio. He based the idea on the laws of electricity and magnetism. Philo figured it was possible to take an image, break it into invisible electronic pieces, and use a magnet to guide the image through a tube. The image would then be recreated

The magazine, Science and Invention, *served as a major influence on Farnsworth's interests as a boy.*

on a screen. Philo Farnsworth had envisioned television.

Philo was excited by his new idea, just as he had been when he came up with the magnetic car key invention. He was anxious to share it with someone who could understand. He chose Mr. Tolman. One day, Philo slipped into an empty

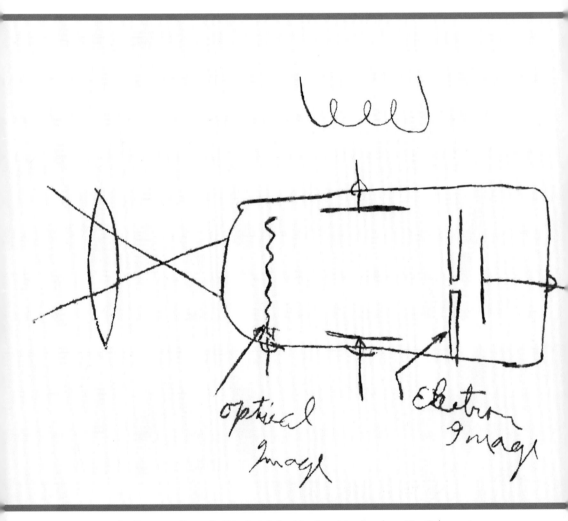

▲ Farnsworth made this sketch for his chemistry teacher, Mr. Tolman, to help describe his idea for electronic television.

classroom and drew a detailed sketch of his idea on the chalkboard. Mr. Tolman came in, and Philo explained the concept. "It just might work," Mr. Tolman said.[5]

Philo always carried a notebook in which he could write down ideas when they struck him. He drew a simple version of his chalkboard sketch on a piece of notebook paper and handed it to Mr. Tolman. Though Philo did not know it at the time, Mr. Tolman kept that sketch for decades.

➲ WORKING AND LEARNING

Philo never completed high school in Idaho. His father moved the family to Provo, Utah, in the fall of 1922. Philo stayed behind in Idaho and found work as a railroad electrician. He worked that job for almost a year, saved his money for college, and joined his family in Utah. But when Philo tried to enroll in Brigham Young University (BYU), there was a problem: Because he had never completed the necessary high school classes that BYU required, the college would not let him in.

Philo instead enrolled as a "special student" at BYU, which allowed him to finish the high school classes he needed. Finally, Philo was allowed to take college math and science classes. He knew he needed the high challenge if he were to someday try to turn his television idea into a reality.

Philo finished his high school requirements through a program provided at Brigham Young University. While there, he (center) acted in the play Charm School.

One of the most valuable experiences Philo had at BYU was working in the school's glass lab. He learned about vacuum tubes, or glass tubes without any air inside. These vacuum tubes would soon become a key piece of early television technology.

⇒ MAN OF THE FAMILY

Philo Farnsworth's life would be dotted with disappointments and heartbreaks. One of the hardest tragedies hit him in early 1924. Lewis Farnsworth caught pneumonia and never recovered.

"Son, I'm leaving you in charge of the family," Lewis told his son from his deathbed. "Take good care of them."

"I will, Papa," Philo said as he grabbed his father's hand. Lewis Farnsworth, only fifty-eight years old, died shortly after.[6]

Philo was seventeen, not quite an adult. Now he was loaded with responsibility: He needed to take care of his four younger siblings and also his mother, who fell into a deep state of depression. Philo dropped out of college. There was no way he could support his family and afford the tuition.

At first, Philo continued his schooling at the U.S. Naval Academy in Annapolis, Maryland. To do that, however, he had to survive eight weeks of boot camp, an exhausting test of physical and mental strength. The days were long and the drills were exhausting. Many of the would-be sailors dropped out. Phil made it through boot camp, but realized he would not enjoy life in the military.

Soon Philo returned home to Utah, and made one significant change. The other guys at boot camp had made fun of his first name by calling him "Fido" instead of "Philo." So he dropped the *o* and from then on was known simply as Phil.

Back home, Phil spent time as a logger, radio repairman, street cleaner, and railroad electrician. He even took a job knocking on doors to sell electrical products. None lasted long or paid well. Eventually, Phil landed a job with a local charitable organization called the Community Chest. One

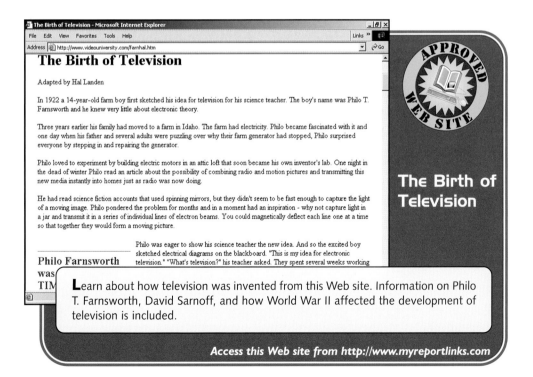

The Birth of Television

Adapted by Hal Landen

In 1922 a 14-year-old farm boy first sketched his idea for television for his science teacher. The boy's name was Philo T. Farnsworth and he knew very little about electronic theory.

Three years earlier his family had moved to a farm in Idaho. The farm had electricity. Philo became fascinated with it and one day when his father and several adults were puzzling over why their farm generator had stopped, Philo surprised everyone by stepping in and repairing the generator.

Philo loved to experiment by building electric motors in an attic loft that soon became his own inventor's lab. One night in the dead of winter Philo read an article about the possibility of combining radio and motion pictures and transmitting this new media instantly into homes just as radio was now doing.

He had read science fiction accounts that used spinning mirrors, but they didn't seem to be fast enough to capture the light of a moving image. Philo pondered the problem for months and in a moment had an inspiration - why not capture light in a jar and transmit it in a series of individual lines of electron beams. You could magnetically deflect each line one at a time so that together they would form a moving picture.

Philo was eager to show his science teacher the new idea. And so the excited boy sketched electrical diagrams on the blackboard. "This is my idea for electronic television." "What's television?" his teacher asked. They spent several weeks working

The Birth of Television

Learn about how television was invented from this Web site. Information on Philo T. Farnsworth, David Sarnoff, and how World War II affected the development of television is included.

Access this Web site from http://www.myreportlinks.com

day, Farnsworth was sitting with Cliff Gardner and the men who ran the Community Chest—George Everson and Leslie Gorrell. Everson asked Phil if he was planning to go back to school. Phil told Everson that he could not afford it but was hoping to find money to fund the development of an idea he had. Everson asked about the idea. Phil told him about television. Phil explained, "It's a way of sending pictures through the air the same way as we do sound."[7]

For the next few days, Gorrell, who was an engineer, mulled the idea. He realized it would probably work. He told Everson this and the two of them decided to invest money that Phil could

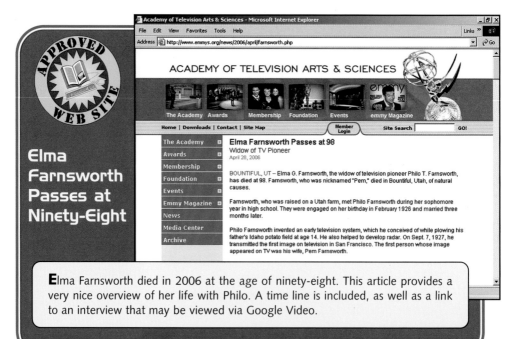

Elma
Farnsworth
Passes at
Ninety-Eight

Academy of Television Arts & Sciences - Microsoft Internet Explorer

File Edit View Favorites Tools Help   Links »

Address http://www.emmys.org/news/2006/april/farnsworth.php   Go

ACADEMY OF TELEVISION ARTS & SCIENCES

The Academy Awards   Membership Foundation   Events   *emmy* Magazine

Home | Downloads | Contact | Site Map   Member Login   Site Search   GO!

The Academy
Awards
Membership
Foundation
Events
Emmy Magazine
News
Media Center
Archive

Elma Farnsworth Passes at 98
Widow of TV Pioneer
April 28, 2006

BOUNTIFUL, UT – Elma G. Farnsworth, the widow of television pioneer Philo T. Farnsworth, has died at 98. Farnsworth, who was nicknamed "Pem," died in Bountiful, Utah, of natural causes.

Farnsworth, who was raised on a Utah farm, met Philo Farnsworth during her sophomore year in high school. They were engaged on her birthday in February 1926 and married three months later.

Philo Farnsworth invented an early television system, which he conceived of while plowing his father's Idaho potato field at age 14. He also helped to develop radar. On Sept. 7, 1927, he transmitted the first image on television in San Francisco. The first person whose image appeared on TV was his wife, Pem Farnsworth.

Elma Farnsworth died in 2006 at the age of ninety-eight. This article provides a very nice overview of her life with Philo. A time line is included, as well as a link to an interview that may be viewed via Google Video.

Access this Web site from http://www.myreportlinks.com

use to develop television from an idea to a reality. Soon, the three men formed a partnership: Everson provided six thousand dollars (a large sum at that time, equal to roughly seventy thousand dollars in 2007); Gorrell provided the support; and Phil the energy.

The new partners decided to open their office in Los Angeles, California. Phil wanted to be near the California Institute of Technology and the Hollywood film industry, which seemed a natural place to develop television.

⊜ Getting Married

By then, Phil was in a serious relationship with a girl named Elma Gardner, who preferred the name "Pem." At age eighteen, she was slightly younger than Phil. They had not had planned to be married, but when the partners decided to move the operation to Los Angeles, Phil wanted Pem to go with him. He called her and said, "Pem, darling, can you be ready to be married in three days?"

"Phil Farnsworth!" she cried. "You've got to be kidding. Of course I can't be married in three days!"[8]

Pem's mother had died four months earlier. Pem felt she needed to stay and help her father take care of her four younger siblings. But Farnsworth convinced Pem's father and his mother that the wedding was a good thing. Philo and Pem Farnsworth were married on a Thursday. The next day they took a train to Los Angeles.

Philo T. Farnsworth spent the first few days doing library research and then setting up his lab. With Pem working at his side, Farnsworth began building his Image Dissector. He ended up with a glass tube that contained an anode and cathode. Current entered the cell through the anode, traveled through the tube, and exited via the cathode. If the Image Dissector worked correctly it would be able to transmit a beam of light. During the summer, Farnsworth invited Everson and Gorrell to see his progress. He demonstrated the Image Dissector the first time for them. But it blew up.

Farnsworth was disappointed. But Gorrell

From left to right: Les Gorrell, Philo Farnsworth, and George Everson.

pointed out that Farnsworth's ideas were still intact. Most inventions fail the first several times they are tried. The partners cleared away the mess, sat at a table, and decided what to do next. They figured they had enough money left to hire a patent attorney, who could register the idea with the United States government. This would be important in the event that Farnsworth ever needed to prove that the idea was his. With the motion picture industry in Los Angeles, there were several such lawyers nearby. Everson found one and had Phil explain his idea. The patent attorney was enthusiastic and encouraged them to continue.

⊜ LOOKING FOR MONEY

The partners figured they needed twenty-five thousand dollars to keep developing the television idea. Everson and Gorrell tried mightily to find interested investors, but struck out everywhere. Looking for advice, Everson went to San Francisco to see a banker named Jesse McCargar. When he arrived at Crocker First National Bank he learned that McCargar was on vacation. Instead, Everson talked to a banker named J. J. Fagan, who seemed interested in Farnsworth's idea. Fagan wanted others to verify that Farnsworth's idea was indeed a good one. He asked to have Farnsworth go to San Francisco to meet with an engineer named Roy Bishop. Farnsworth met with Bishop, and then gave another presentation to another engineer, Harlan Honn. Honn was convinced that television would work. When McCargar returned to town, he accepted the idea as well, which led to the formation of a new company. The bankers owned 60 percent, Everson and Gorrell 10 percent each, and Farnsworth held 20 percent. The new company would be based out of San Francisco.

The Dream and the Realities of Business

In September 1926, Phil and Pem Farnsworth packed up the contents of their Los Angeles apartment and drove north to San Francisco. Once there, they set up a workshop in an area called Telegraph Hill. Farnsworth hired Cliff Gardner as an assistant in the lab. Gardner learned how to make the glass tubes they needed to test the Image Dissector, and they began conducting experiments. Farnsworth led the process and Gardner assisted. Pem used drafting equipment to draw detailed pictures of the equipment and a typewriter to transcribe her husband's detailed notes.

Farnsworth soon realized that he needed to apply for a patent. He did that with the help of his lawyer, Donald Lippincott, who was also an engineer. Getting the patents would allow Farnsworth to make sure nobody could steal his ideas

CHAPTER 3

outright. On the other hand, other inventors could learn about his ideas and try to find ways to improve them. So getting the patent added protection *and* pressure to market the invention before the patents ran out and others could.

Throughout 1927, Farnsworth moved fast. The staff worked twelve hours a day, six days a week. At first, more things seemed to go wrong than right. But Farnsworth knew this was part of the invention process. He once told Pem, "I'm a professional mistake maker."[1]

Farnsworth's history of misfires made the success on the morning of September 7, 1927 even sweeter. When Gardner placed that slide in front of the Image Dissector and the line appeared moments later on the reception set, Farnsworth's progress was clear. He had made mistakes, but he had learned from them. Much work remained, but Farnsworth now knew that electronic television could—and *would*—become reality.

Cliff Gardner holds one of the tubes used to test Farnsworth's early television system. Gardner made the tubes by blowing fiery hot glass.

→ BANKING ON THE DEMONSTRATION

In early 1928, Farnsworth kept solving problems, one after another. He improved the resolution—making images less fuzzy and more crisp. Later that year, he invited the bankers for a demonstration. He began by showing them a dollar sign on a blue screen. "Here's something a banker will understand," he said. His audience laughed. Farnsworth also had Cliff Gardner smoke a cigarette. The moving smoke came through on the screen. The bankers began talking about selling the company

IEEEVM: Farnsworth's Image Dissector - Microsoft Internet Explorer

File   Edit   View   Favorites   Tools   Help   Links »

Address http://ieee-virtual-museum.org/collection/tech.php?id=2345850&lid=1

Farnsworth's Image Dissector

The 1927 version of Farnsworth's image dissector. He received a patent for the image dissector in 1930, and successfully defended that patent against Vladimir Zworykin and David Sarnoff. Courtesy: Smithsonian Institution.

Philo T. Farnsworth, one of the pioneers of electronic television, invented a special type of electron tube for use as a camera tube or imaging tube in television systems. This tube, for which he filed a patent in 1927, was called the Image Dissector. To understand how an Image Dissector works, it is best to simplify the concept. In the simplification, the image dissector "sees" the outside world through a glass lens, which focused an image through the clear glass wall of the tube on a special plate, which was coated with a ... cessium oxide. When light strik... oxide, it emits electrons, so yo... the special plate like a mirror that "reflects" an image made of elect... than light. This invisible electron "reflection" was aimed at a small de... which captured the electrons so that they could be amplified and transm... tele...

Farnsworth's Image Dissector was an early electronic television camera tube that he successfully demonstrated and made patent applications for in 1927. See a photograph of the invention when you visit this Web site.

EDITOR'S CHOICE

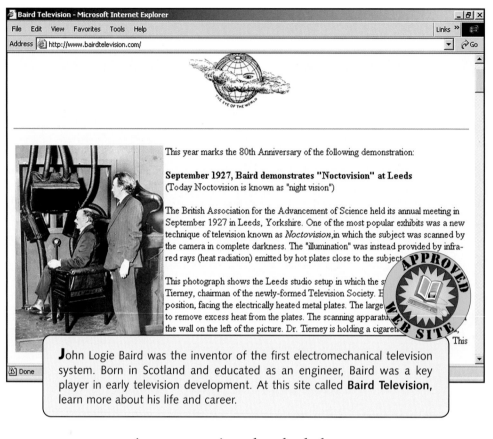

Baird Television - Microsoft Internet Explorer

File   Edit   View   Favorites   Tools   Help   Links »

Address http://www.bairdtelevision.com/   Go

This year marks the 80th Anniversary of the following demonstration:

September 1927, Baird demonstrates "Noctovision" at Leeds
(Today Noctovision is known as "night vision")

The British Association for the Advancement of Science held its annual meeting in September 1927 in Leeds, Yorkshire. One of the most popular exhibits was a new technique of television known as *Noctovision,* in which the subject was scanned by the camera in complete darkness. The "illumination" was instead provided by infra-red rays (heat radiation) emitted by hot plates close to the subject.

This photograph shows the Leeds studio setup in which the s[...] Tierney, chairman of the newly-formed Television Society. [...] position, facing the electrically heated metal plates. The large[...] to remove excess heat from the plates. The scanning apparat[...] the wall on the left of the picture. Dr. Tierney is holding a cigaret[...]

This

Done

John Logie Baird was the inventor of the first electromechanical television system. Born in Scotland and educated as an engineer, Baird was a key player in early television development. At this site called **Baird Television,** learn more about his life and career.

to a major corporation that had the resources to fully develop television.[2]

While the newspapers covered the development of mechanical television, Farnsworth's work remained fairly quiet. That changed, though, on September 1, 1928, when Farnsworth held a press conference to show off his work. He explained the concept of electronic television. To give reporters a firsthand look at how it worked, he showed a film clip of an actress named Mary Pickford combing her hair in *The Taming of the Shrew.* A reporter named Earle Ennis from the *San Francisco Chronicle* wrote a story for the Monday paper with the headline: "S.F. Man's Invention to Revolutionize Television." The large photo that accompanied the story made Farnsworth appear much older than his twenty-two years: The hair atop his long, narrow face was slicked back and he had grown a mustache, giving him a smart, mature look. He wore a suit and held the Image Dissector and television receiving tubes. Ennis referred to Farnsworth as a "young genius." Newspapers across the country picked up on the story.[3]

In New York City, a man named David Sarnoff read about Farnsworth. Sarnoff was head of the Radio Corporation of America (RCA). His company made millions of dollars from the sale of radios. Sarnoff was concerned that television could hurt the radio business. He decided that if television was the future, RCA would be the company to bring it to the world. Then and there, Sarnoff decided to keep a close watch on this young inventor named Farnsworth.

Fire!

In late October 1928, Farnsworth and Pem were playing tennis with Cliff and Lola Gardner when a policeman approached Farnsworth and said, "You might want to get down to your laboratory right away. The place is on fire!" They all loaded into the

David Sarnoff at a function in 1966. Sarnoff was the head of RCA who desperately wanted his company to be the worldwide leader in television making.

policeman's car and headed to the laboratory. They quickly saw that the lab was burnt down to nothing.[4]

Farnsworth found out the next day that the lab was insured and could be rebuilt. Pem had brought the lab journals home, so they were safe. These journals were important recordings of Farnsworth's scientific work. The staff was back at work in a new and improved lab in early December.

Around the same time, the company was reorganized and given a new name, Television Laboratories. The bankers held shares of stock in the company, as did Farnsworth, Everson, and Gorrell. The bankers asked that Pem quit so that the operation would seem more professional. Back then, having your wife work for you made it seem like you had a very small operation. She did quit, and after working a short time at a factory, quit that job, too. Farnsworth's stock in the company was enough to buy them a nice new car, house, and piano. He gave shares to family members, including his mother. Mrs. Farnsworth temporarily moved in with Phil and Pem. When their first son, also named Philo, was born in September 1929, Mrs. Farnsworth was there to help Pem.

⇒ TOUGH FINANCIAL TIMES

The stock market crashed in October 1929. That meant the value of American business was dropping quickly. This left Television Laboratories'

This is the Farnsworth Television Receiver circa 1930. The white circle is the screen that displays the image.

bankers desperate for money. McCargar tried to close Television Laboratories, insisting the bankers could not pour any more money into it. He wanted to shut it down until a buyer could be found. Farnsworth protested so angrily that he almost punched McCargar. Everson suggested that the employees be given stock in the company instead of salaries, and McCargar agreed. Television Laboratories could remain open, for now.

Farnsworth's work continued to receive publicity, and the quality of his invention improved. He could now transmit signals a mile away. His staff built seven-inch circular screens that were mounted inside wooden cabinets. Visitors kept

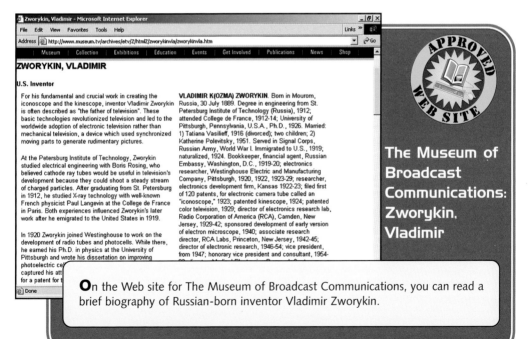

On the Web site for The Museum of Broadcast Communications, you can read a brief biography of Russian-born inventor Vladimir Zworykin.

Access this Web site from http://www.myreportlinks.com

coming to see Farnsworth's work, including radio inventor Guglielmo Marconi and Herbert Hoover, Jr., son of the president. Actors Douglas Fairbanks, Sr., and his wife, Mary Pickford, also stopped by. (Pickford was the actress who Farnsworth showed combing her hair during his press conference.)

However, McCargar and Everson, the bankers, wanted a visitor with the money power to buy Television Laboratories. So, they were excited when a visit was scheduled for Vladimir Zworykin, head of television research at Westinghouse Electric Corporation. Farnsworth was excited, too, but not because he hoped Westinghouse would buy his company. Instead, he wanted to license his work to Westinghouse. That would mean that

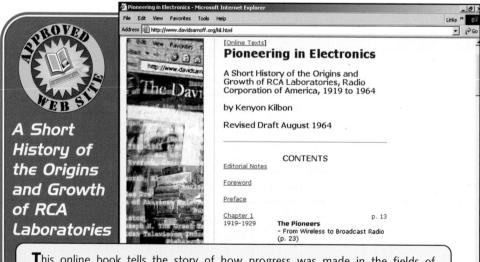

A Short History of the Origins and Growth of RCA Laboratories

[Online Texts]

Pioneering in Electronics

A Short History of the Origins and Growth of RCA Laboratories, Radio Corporation of America, 1919 to 1964

by Kenyon Kilbon

Revised Draft August 1964

CONTENTS

Editorial Notes

Foreword

Preface

Chapter 1   p. 13
1919-1929   **The Pioneers**
                   - From Wireless to Broadcast Radio
                   (p. 23)

This online book tells the story of how progress was made in the fields of electronics and industrial research, with a history of RCA as the backdrop. From wireless to broadcast radio, to early television and radar, decades of RCA research is covered.

Access this Web site from http://www.myreportlinks.com

Westinghouse would pay Farnsworth a fee to make and distribute his inventions. Farnsworth was also aware of Zworykin's work on electronic receiving tubes and was excited to have a knowledgeable visitor.

The staff showed Zworykin every courtesy when he visited in April 1930, explaining their inventions and processes in detail. He spent three days absorbing all of Farnsworth's work. He asked for, and received, a demonstration of how an Image Dissector was built from scratch. "This is a splendid instrument," Zworykin said, holding the Image Dissector. "I wish I would have invented it myself."[5]

THE VISITOR IS A SPY!

What Farnsworth did not realize was this: Zworykin had recently been hired by RCA. His job? Develop television. Zworykin was visiting Farnsworth's laboratory to secretly collect information. In other words, he was spying.

Directly after visiting Farnsworth, Zworykin returned to his Pittsburgh lab, built an Image Dissector as best he could from memory, then packed and went to New York to see RCA president David Sarnoff.

This spying continued in the spring and summer of 1930. Two visitors from RCA spent time at Farnsworth's lab, then followed up with a letter to Farnsworth asking for models of his work. Farnsworth's investors grew suspicious and investigated the situation. They deduced that RCA was trying to steal their ideas.

This was part of Sarnoff's plan to ensure that RCA would emerge as the leader in television. Farnsworth had already beaten RCA to the invention. In August 1930, the U.S. government granted his patents for a television scanning system and a television receiving system. Those patents were official proof that Farnsworth was

The American Experience/Technology/Big Dream Small Screen - Microsoft Internet Explorer

File   Edit   View   Favorites   Tools   Help   Links »

Address http://www.pbs.org/wgbh/amex/technology/bigdream/   Go

WHO WE ARE | SCHEDULE | ARCHIVES | KIDS | TEACHERS | CONTACT US | SHOP

AM≋RICAN
EXPERIENCE

Technology Home

About the Program
TV Milestones
More about Sarnoff
Read More Learn More
Teacher's Guide

BIG DREAM
SMALL SCREEN

Technology Timeline

Sites
Sky"
hone"

APPROVED WEB SITE

The **"Big Dream Small Screen"** site contains a time line of TV milestones, an interactive technology time line, a biography of David Sarnoff, and the story behind the battle that waged between Philo T. Farnsworth and David Sarnoff to control the development of television.

the inventor of television technology. The patents also meant that any company that wanted to use Farnsworth's technology would have to pay him.

Still, the patents were only a start. Transforming television from an idea to a product was an entirely different challenge. People needed to buy televisions for their homes. For that to happen, televisions needed to be mass-produced and available in stores. Of course, there also needed to be something to watch on television.

Accomplishing both these tasks—creating television programming and producing television sets to be sold—would take massive amounts of money. During that time, however, the Farnsworth company was cutting back. McCargar sliced the budget and Farnsworth had to let go his three best engineers.

Manpower and money. Farnsworth did not have it—but RCA did.

⇨ Time Starts Ticking

Farnsworth's patents would be good for seventeen years. After that, his ideas would become freely available to any person or company that wanted to use them. So his best chance to make massive amounts of money from television was between 1930 and the year the key patents were scheduled to expire—1947.

Seventeen years may seem like a long time, but when you consider how far television was from

This photo was transmitted via television at the Philo T. Farnsworth Television Laboratories in Philadelphia. The transmission took place in 1935.

becoming a common technology, it was not. Because television was to be broadcast through the air, and the American people essentially owned the airwaves, the government had to give permission for television broadcasts to be aired nationwide. That had not happened yet.

In December 1930, Farnsworth testified to the Federal Radio Commission, urging them to let companies broadcast television shows and sell television sets. But David Sarnoff used all of his influence to work against Farnsworth. He convinced government officials to hold off on approving television. That may seem strange because Sarnoff, like Farnsworth, wanted to get into the television business. But if Sarnoff did enter television, RCA would have had to pay for the use of Farnsworth's patents. Sarnoff hated the very idea. "RCA doesn't pay royalties," he said. "We collect them!"[6]

Tied Up in Court

Instead, RCA's strategy was to stall Farnsworth. The company had the money and power to do it. Sarnoff had RCA's lawyers challenge Farnsworth's patents in court, even though the corporation had little chance of winning: Farnsworth was clearly the inventor of electronic television. But what Sarnoff really wanted to do was buy time. While Farnsworth's time and energy was tied up in court,

Zworykin and other RCA workers were developing their own television technology.

SARNOFF PAYS A VISIT

In April 1931, Sarnoff made arrangements to visit Farnsworth's lab. Farnsworth was not there for the visit, which was handled by George Everson, Cliff Gardner, and some of the staff. They demonstrated the television system. Soon after Sarnoff's visit, Everson received an offer from RCA to buy the entire company for $100,000. The offer was terribly low—investors had already spent that much building the company. Farnsworth, who was in New York, rejected the offer. So did the bankers, who were hoping for an offer in the range of $500,000 to $1 million.

It was clear that Sarnoff simply wanted to buy out Farnsworth. That would get rid of the competition and put Farnsworth to work for him.

With the offer rejected, Sarnoff took a different approach: He increased RCA's investment in television development to $1 million per year. If he could not buy Farnsworth's company, he would simply try to outspend it, and develop products to be ready when Farnsworth's patents expired.

Sarnoff had patience and RCA had money. Meanwhile, time was ticking away on Farnsworth's patents.[7]

⊜ MOVE TO PHILADELPHIA

In May 1931, Phil and Pem celebrated their fifth wedding anniversary in New York. They went to a fancy dinner, attended a Yankees game the next day, visited the Statue of Liberty, and took an elevator to the top of the Alfred Smith Building, now called the Empire State Building.

Then Phil and Pem boarded a train with Jesse McCargar for Philadelphia, where executives from Philco, the largest radio manufacturer in the world, wanted to make a deal. Philco's number one competitor was RCA. For Philco executives, making a deal with Farnsworth Laboratories would open up the new market of television. The companies reached an agreement by which Philco would license TV technology from Farnsworth. The Farnsworth Laboratories would move to Philadelphia and so would Phil, Pem, and their sons Philo, Jr., age one, and infant Kenny.

The Farnsworths moved to Philadelphia in July 1931. Philco kept the arrangement top secret. Just across the Delaware River in Camden, New Jersey, Zworykin and RCA engineers were working on television as well. Soon the two competitors could keep track of each other's progress through experimental television station broadcasts. At one point, Philco had a camera focused on the University of Pennsylvania swimming pool. An engineer from RCA called and said, "You know your camera at the swimming pool? Do you know some of the students are swimming without bathing suits?"[8] Clearly, that camera needed to be moved.

⊙ TOUGH TIMES

For all of his achievements as a young man, Farnsworth's life was crammed with challenges and misfortunes. In 1932, when the economy of the United States was crumbling, the Farnsworths' bank closed down. One day earlier, Farnsworth had made a huge deposit of money.

Using articles, photographs, and videos, the **Farnovision** Web site provides a detailed account of the life of Philo T. Farnsworth and his struggles to realize his dream.

EDITOR'S CHOICE

As a result, Farnsworth and Pem lost almost all of their money.

But that was not the worst part of 1932 for the family. In March, the Farnsworths' eighteen-month-old son, Kenny, developed a throat infection. Doctors' medicines back then were not nearly as effective as they are now, and the infection grew worse. Kenny never recovered.

Phil and Pem were devastated by their son's death. They decided to bury him in Utah, but Farnsworth's bosses at Philco would not let him take the time off to travel there. So Pem went back to Utah without him to bury Kenny. Farnsworth was lonely and heartbroken. In the months that followed, Phil and Pem's marriage, once a loving friendship, had grown distant and cold. Phil Farnsworth developed an ulcer, or a bleeding on the lining of his stomach that is often caused by stress. He started drinking to fight the pain. His life and health were in shambles.

The one thing he kept on track, however, was television. Farnsworth never lost his focus on that.

Who Invented Television?

Farnsworth split free from Philco in the summer of 1933. Back on his own, he continued to work on developing television technology. At the same time, Everson began meeting with businesspeople trying to convince them to purchase stock in Farnsworth Television.

Farnsworth's goal during this time was to convince electronics manufacturers to buy the rights to make televisions. By selling licenses to his work, Farnsworth could ensure himself of making money both in the present and in the future, when he believed televisions would become more popular. But he was having difficulty actually getting manufacturers to buy into his work. Farnsworth noticed that people seemed to believe RCA was far ahead in its work on television. He knew this was

In November 1934, *Modern Mechanix and Innovations* magazine published an article on Philo Farnsworth and television. You can view a copy of the original pages when you visit the **Perfected Television** Web site.

not true. But Farnsworth also knew that RCA was determined to catch up.

RCA was turning millions of dollars in profit by selling radios. Little was said publicly about television, but RCA was spending millions of dollars on developing the technology. A transmitter was placed on the top of the Empire State Building and an experimental station was constructed inside the National Broadcasting Company (NBC)'s Radio City office.

FARNSWORTH PROVES HIS INVENTION

Meanwhile, when Farnsworth would make a public presentation about television, the information always seemed to find its way back to competitors like RCA. Farnsworth decided to fight this by asking the U.S. Patent Office to decide once and for all who invented television.[9]

Farnsworth's attorney, Donald Lippincott, needed to prove that his client had come up with the idea for television first. He knew it to be true—Farnsworth had visualized the Image Dissector at age fourteen. But Farnsworth had told only two people: his father, who was dead, and Justin Tolman, his teacher.

Lippincott set out on a search for Tolman. He found him retired in Salt Lake City, Utah. He asked if Tolman remembered Philo Farnsworth. "I surely do. Brightest student I ever had." It turned out

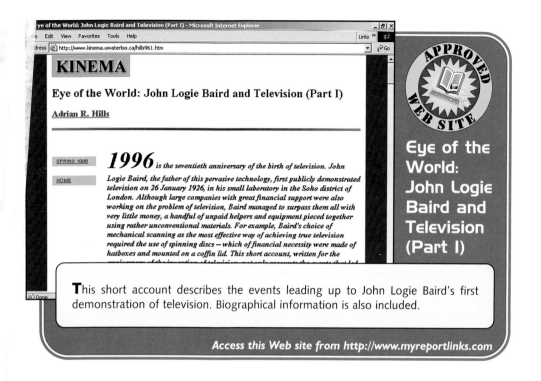

KINEMA

Eye of the World: John Logie Baird and Television (Part I)

Adrian R. Hills

SPRING 1996

HOME

1996 *is the seventieth anniversary of the birth of television. John Logie Baird, the father of this pervasive technology, first publicly demonstrated television on 26 January 1926, in his small laboratory in the Soho district of London. Although large companies with great financial support were also working on the problem of television, Baird managed to surpass them all with very little money, a handful of unpaid helpers and equipment pieced together using rather unconventional materials. For example, Baird's choice of mechanical scanning as the most effective way of achieving true television required the use of spinning discs – which of financial necessity were made of hatboxes and mounted on a coffin lid. This short account, written for the*

Eye of the World: John Logie Baird and Television (Part I)

This short account describes the events leading up to John Logie Baird's first demonstration of television. Biographical information is also included.

Access this Web site from http://www.myreportlinks.com

that Tolman had told years' worth of students about Farnsworth's genius idea and let them know that the concept of electronic television had been first created in Rigby, Utah.[10]

When testifying during the trial, Tolman told of the blackboard drawing Farnsworth had done for him. He also pulled from his shirt pocket the simple notebook-paper sketch Farnsworth had made for him.

While waiting for a decision on who invented television, Farnsworth showed off his technology to as many people as he could. He invited back Mary Pickford, who was impressed by the improved quality of the transmission. He also participated in a ten-day demonstration at a Philadelphia science museum called the Franklin Institute.

In late July 1935, a document arrived from the U.S. Patent Office. It concluded that Farnsworth was indeed the person who invented television. This was a victory for Farnsworth. Still, his clash with RCA was far from over.[11]

⊜ Times Turn Hot

In late 1936, the Farnsworths traveled to London. Their relationship was happier now than it had been a few years earlier. They were eager for time together. During the day, Farnsworth helped businessman John Logie Baird set up an electronic television system. At night, he and Pem enjoyed dinner and dancing. They then traveled to the French Riveria where they wanted to spend the holidays. But Baird sent them a telegram containing bad news: A fire in the Crystal Palace, where Baird stored all of his equipment, had caused the entire television system to burn.

This was yet another setback for Farnsworth, who was accustomed to tough luck. But it was not the most nerve-racking part of his European trip. While visiting Germany, Farnsworth found himself in a meeting with a Nazi official. The Nazis, led by Adolf Hitler, had taken control of Germany and were preparing to invade the rest of Europe.

Philo Taylor Farnsworth (1906-1971) invented the current system of television transmission and reception at his 202 Green Street laboratory, and it can be said it was one of the great scientific inventions of the 20th century. It is all more remarkable because the young inventor had recently celebrated his 22nd birthday when this Chronicle article was published that told of his television breakthrough.

The article names Leslie Gorrell, George Everson, William W. Crocker, and Roy N. Bishop as supporting, and

APPROVED WEB SITE

Farnsworth had just celebrated his twenty-second birthday when reporters from the *San Francisco Chronicle* visited his Green Street laboratory to discuss the inventor's major advances in television. Read the original article here at a Web page called **Inventor Philo Taylor Farnsworth (1906–1971).**

EDITOR'S CHOICE

Bright minds were in huge demand—the Nazis wanted talented people working for their cause. That included scientists. Making the situation worse, the Nazis were known to use threats and even violence to get what they wanted.

When Phil and Pem tried to leave Germany, the paperwork they needed for departure was delayed. Nervous and worried, they badly wanted to go home. Pem later wrote that the Farnsworths were certain that Hitler himself was keeping track of their whereabouts.

Phil and Pem finally escaped Germany, taking a train in the middle of the night and a ship back to New York.[12]

⇨ LOOKING FOR A BREAK

Back in the United States, Farnsworth's company was not nearly as profitable as its investors wanted it to be. On April 1, 1937, Jesse McCargar walked into Farnsworth's office and told him to fire the employees in an effort to cut costs. When Farnsworth refused, McCargar went into the lab and did it himself. "You're all fired!" he said. "Pack up your stuff and leave."[13]

Farnsworth decided to try to raise enough money to buy the portion of the company owned by McCargar and the other Crocker Bank investors. George Everson began working on finding new investors. By the spring of 1938, they were still working on a deal. The stock market was shaky because investors were nervous about the potential effects of war. (Hitler's Germany had just taken over Austria.) Farnsworth needed to get away. He and Pem, with Cliff and Lola Gardner, took a trip to Maine. Farnsworth ended up buying an old farm in Fryeburg, Maine.

In March 1939, the federal government granted approval for the Farnsworth Television & Radio Corporation to become a public company. That meant investors could buy stock in the company.

The company raised $3 million this way and bought out McCarger.

Meanwhile, David Sarnoff of RCA decided to make a big publicity splash. In April, during the 1939 World's Fair in New York City, he staged a grand spectacle, announcing that the era of television had begun. The first black-and-white sets were going on sale for the hefty price of six hundred dollars. (Soon, more basic TVs would be on sale for as low as $150.) NBC began airing television shows.

Sarnoff never mentioned Zworykin or Farnsworth. He took credit himself and then gave the podium to President Franklin D. Roosevelt. The

Included on the Web site is an online handbook to help inventors learn about the business of inventing, with information on raising capital and applying for patents. A searchable "Inventor of the Week" archives is available, as well as games and trivia quizzes, inventor biographies, and links to online invention resources.

Access this Web site from http://www.myreportlinks.com

scene was playing in department store windows throughout New York City. People stopped on the sidewalks to watch. Farnsworth figured then and there that Sarnoff would be known as the pioneer of television.

He was right.[14]

⊛ DEALING WITH RCA

In early 1939, Edwin "Nick" Nicholas was hired to lead the Farnsworth company. Nicholas had formerly worked at RCA and knew Sarnoff well. Nicholas was confident that RCA needed to license Farnsworth's patents in order to get into the television business. Otherwise, RCA would have to wait until 1947, when Farnsworth's key patents expired.[15]

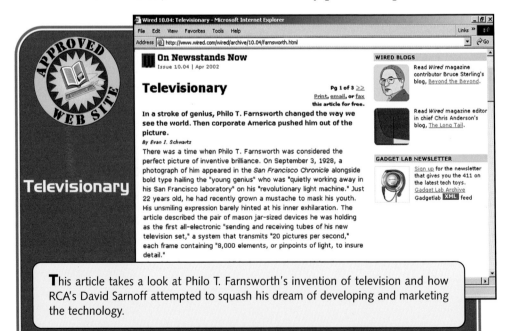

Televisionary

This article takes a look at Philo T. Farnsworth's invention of television and how RCA's David Sarnoff attempted to squash his dream of developing and marketing the technology.

Access this Web site from http://www.myreportlinks.com

When Sarnoff unveiled television at the World's Fair, Farnsworth company officials were furious. They thought, How can Sarnoff do this? RCA does not even have the patents! Nicholas advised against suing RCA. Instead, he said it would be better to reach a licensing deal.

Beginning in May 1939, Nicholas began negotiating with RCA patent chief Otto Schairer. After four months, they reached an agreement: RCA paid Farnsworth $1 million, plus royalties for every television sold. Schairer, some say, cried as he signed the agreement. The deal got little attention in the media, probably because RCA did not want it well-known that it was paying a royalty instead of receiving them.

⇒ THE DISAPPOINTMENTS CONTINUE

In 1939, the Farnsworths moved to the Midwest. His company had purchased a radio plant in Fort Wayne, Indiana, and transferred operations there.

Meanwhile, television manufacturers and government officials were working on a complicated set of rules that would determine the frequency of channels and the resolution of the screens. The government settled on the regulations in 1941, which should have set companies like RCA and Farnsworth free to manufacture television sets, sell them, and start making money. But in December 1941, Japan attacked an American military base in Pearl Harbor, Hawaii. The United States immediately entered World War II. All materials that could have been used to make televisions were redirected to become war supplies. Most broadcasting stopped. For as long as the war lasted, television would have to wait.

Farnsworth realized that his most valuable patents were likely to expire before television became wildly popular. That meant he would not be able to cash in on the technology he had created. This depressed him. He started drinking day and night and began smoking. He turned sicker and lost weight, falling to only one hundred pounds. Although a doctor from Boston helped

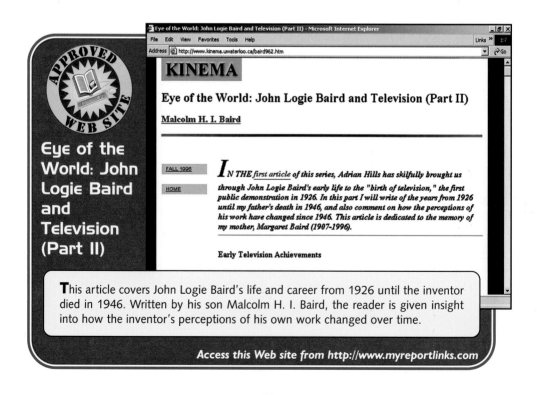

Eye of the World: John Logie Baird and Television (Part II)

KINEMA

Eye of the World: John Logie Baird and Television (Part II)

Malcolm H. I. Baird

FALL 1996

HOME

*I*N THE *first article* of this series, Adrian Hills has skilfully brought us through John Logie Baird's early life to the "birth of television," the first public demonstration in 1926. In this part I will write of the years from 1926 until my father's death in 1946, and also comment on how the perceptions of his work have changed since 1946. This article is dedicated to the memory of my mother, Margaret Baird (1907-1996).

Early Television Achievements

This article covers John Logie Baird's life and career from 1926 until the inventor died in 1946. Written by his son Malcolm H. I. Baird, the reader is given insight into how the inventor's perceptions of his own work changed over time.

Access this Web site from http://www.myreportlinks.com

him recover, Farnsworth struggled with his health for the rest of his life.

Farnsworth's fears proved true: World War II lasted until 1945, only two years before Farnsworth's key patents expired. Television became popular in the very late 1940s, but by then it was too late. Farnsworth's most important patents were available to anyone.

LIFE AFTER THE ARRIVAL OF TELEVISION

High School Musical, American Idol, the Super Bowl—how are these linked? They are all hugely popular shows—and without television, they probably would not even exist.

Television connects our world. When big news happens, say, in the Middle East, virtually everyone in North America knows about it within minutes. Global television networks like CNN have reporters and cameramen on site to capture the news and deliver it to viewers everywhere.

CHAPTER 4

Likewise, when a hurricane is poised to strike the Florida coastline, or a blizzard is headed for the Northeast, television weathercasters can deliver advance warnings.

That is what Philo Farnsworth had in mind when he built the Image Dissector and broadcast the first television picture. He wanted to create a technology that would give people useful information quickly.

⇨ **AT THAT, HE SUCCEEDED.**

But television has had another consequence, one Farnsworth did not intend. The technology became so popular that the average person spends more than four and a half hours each day watching television. The average American home has as many televisions as people.

That is amazing growth. In 1936, approximately two hundred television sets were operated worldwide. By 1948, that number grew to 1 million in the United States alone.[1] But both of those figures pale in comparison to 2001, when the United States government reported 248 million television sets in American homes.[2] In 1948, there were about

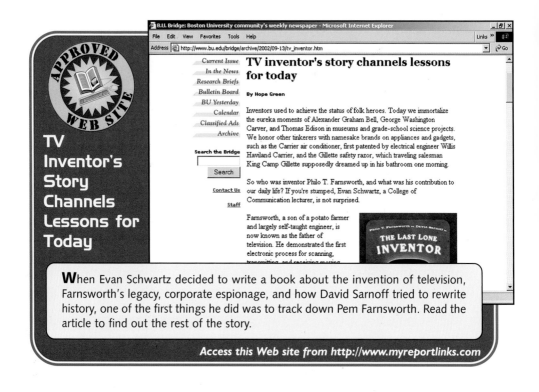

TV
Inventor's
Story
Channels
Lessons for
Today

B.U. Bridge: Boston University community's weekly newspaper - Microsoft Internet Explorer

File   Edit   View   Favorites   Tools   Help

Address   http://www.bu.edu/bridge/archive/2002/09-13/tv_inventor.htm

Current Issue
In the News
Research Briefs
Bulletin Board
BU Yesterday
Calendar
Classified Ads
Archive

Search the Bridge

Search

Contact Us

Staff

TV inventor's story channels lessons for today

By Hope Green

Inventors used to achieve the status of folk heroes. Today we immortalize the eureka moments of Alexander Graham Bell, George Washington Carver, and Thomas Edison in museums and grade-school science projects. We honor other tinkerers with namesake brands on appliances and gadgets, such as the Carrier air conditioner, first patented by electrical engineer Willis Haviland Carrier, and the Gillette safety razor, which traveling salesman King Camp Gillette supposedly dreamed up in his bathroom one morning.

So who was inventor Philo T. Farnsworth, and what was his contribution to our daily life? If you're stumped, Evan Schwartz, a College of Communication lecturer, is not surprised.

Farnsworth, a son of a potato farmer and largely self-taught engineer, is now known as the father of television. He demonstrated the first electronic process for scanning, transmitting, and receiving moving

THE LAST LONE INVENTOR

When Evan Schwartz decided to write a book about the invention of television, Farnsworth's legacy, corporate espionage, and how David Sarnoff tried to rewrite history, one of the first things he did was to track down Pem Farnsworth. Read the article to find out the rest of the story.

Access this Web site from http://www.myreportlinks.com

154 million people in the United States, and in 2000 there were 298 million in the United States. That means that in 1948 there was about one television for every 154 people. In 2001, there was roughly one television for every 1.2 people.

→A GROWING INDUSTRY

At the end of World War II, the television industry exploded in popularity.

People were hungry for news and entertainment. Manufacturers that had been busy for years making military equipment could now focus on making things like televisions. Families were ready to buy, often spending several hundred dollars for a single set. Neighbors and relatives who did not have TV sets often dropped by the homes of those who did.

Though the public paid for television sets, they did not pay for television shows—those were free. But the networks NBC, ABC, and CBS and their local stations needed to make money. They did so by selling advertising. There was no better way for companies to get their products in front of people than putting them on television. For example, the food company Kraft sponsored an NBC show called *Kraft Television Theater.* It advertised a product called Cheez Whiz, which people started buying in massive amounts.

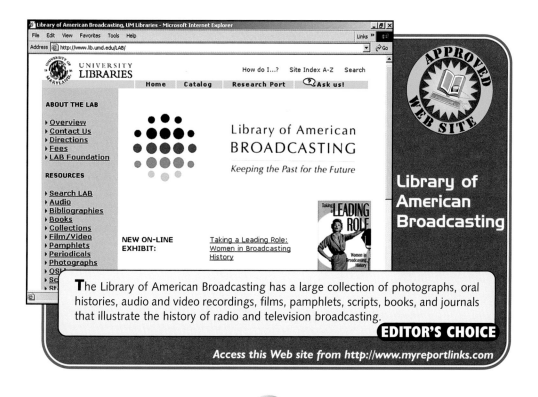

The Library of American Broadcasting has a large collection of photographs, oral histories, audio and video recordings, films, pamphlets, scripts, books, and journals that illustrate the history of radio and television broadcasting.

EDITOR'S CHOICE

Access this Web site from http://www.myreportlinks.com

Advertising remains the most important way that television networks make money. The cost of buying a thirty second Super Bowl advertisement in 2007 was as high as $2.6 million. (Super Bowl commercials are usually the costliest of all advertisements.)[3] But not all television remains free to the public. While anyone can receive basic network channels like NBC, CBS, ABC, and Fox at no cost, stations like ESPN, MTV, and CNN cost money. That is because they are only available by cable or satellite.

The **Early Television Foundation** is a nonprofit organization that collects and restores early television equipment and memorabilia. The museum has one of the best collections of television receivers in the United States. Learn more about early television from this site.

Cable television was developed in the 1950s to help customers who lived in places where broadcast signals could not reach. Those customers received their television stations through a cable line that strung directly into their home, just as a telephone line did. At first, cable customers received exactly the same channels as non-cable viewers. But by the end of the 1950s, cable companies started adding extra channels that customers could not receive with just a television and antenna.

Hundreds of Channels

During the next three decades, cable television boomed. Specialty stations like Home Box Office (HBO), ESPN, MTV, Nickelodeon, and CNN became available. Customers were willing to pay extra money to receive those, so even more stations were created. Today, customers can buy hundreds of channels that touch almost any topic, from food to weather to golf. They can receive them through cables or by using a satellite dish that receives a signal beamed from space.

In 1952, only fourteen thousand people received cable television. By 2005, 92 million households subscribed to cable. Those numbers prove this: People love television, and they are willing to pay for it.[4]

⇒ SCREEN ATTRACTION

Television has a magical ability: Viewers feel a real connection with the person on the screen—even if they have never met. That attraction has helped shape history.

Many historians believe that television helped John F. Kennedy become president of the United States. In 1960, Kennedy was running against Richard Nixon. The two men faced off in the first-ever televised presidential debate. Kennedy was a young senator; Nixon was the vice president of the United States. Based on that alone, Nixon was likely more qualified for the presidency. But voters do not choose presidents solely on experience. Charm matters, too. Television gave voters a chance to see a stark difference between the candidates: Kennedy was smiling and likeable, handsome and polished. Nixon appeared nervous and uncomfortable on camera. One performance was smooth; the other was shaky. Kennedy won the election.

Since then, a business called media coaching has developed. Media coaches offer training to politicians, celebrities, athletes, and anyone else who regularly appears on television. The coaches teach their clients how to look into a camera, speak clearly, and give short, lively answers for the audience.

Television has also changed the way that people view celebrities. Before television, singers and

They were some of early television's first writers, directors, producers, and production assistants. The spotlight is at long last focused on some of the women who helped to invent television in postwar New York. Read their biographies at the **Missing in Action: The Women Behind Television's Golden Age** online resource.

actors were famous, but they were not nearly as recognizable as they are now. Television shows thrust famous faces in front of viewers every day. The exposure is so frequent that fans now have a huge interest in celebrities' personal lives.

Consider the example of actor Michael J. Fox, who is famous for his roles in television shows such as *Family Ties* and *Spin City* and also for the *Back to the Future* movies. When Fox and his wife, Tracy Pollan, got married in Vermont, reporters wanted to cover the event. Michael and Tracy wanted to limit the wedding to their immediate family and close friends—certainly no microphones and cameras! What followed was an all-out war for their privacy.

During the week before the wedding, reporters and photographers tried almost *anything* to get information. Reporters offered money to hotel employees in exchange for information on the Fox wedding. One dishonest man pretended to be Bill Fox, Michael's father. Another reporter tried to convince Tracy's eighty-two-year-old grandmother to get into his car and give information.

To try to get photos of the wedding, which was taking place outdoors at a mountain inn, photographers dressed in camouflage and hid in the woods. Next door to the inn was a llama farm. One reporter attempted to rent a llama costume to get close to the ceremony. During the day of the wedding, some photographers rented helicopters and flew them over the inn, hoping to get a shot.

Though he knew posing for a photograph or two might get the reporters to stop harassing him and his family, Fox never gave in. The wedding ceremony was held under a tent so the helicopters could not get a shot of it. Not a single image was made public.[5]

Idol Realities

Television has also made people hungry to become famous. That has spawned a new type of show called reality TV. In reality television, average people

▲ *A television studio at the Capitol Radio Engineering Institute in 1945.*

get the chance to compete for a prize on a show. When these average people get on TV, they, too, become celebrities.

Consider the example of John Stevens. In 2004, the sixteen-year-old Stevens was a finalist on the Fox singing show *American Idol*. Stevens was from Buffalo, New York, where he was known as a nice kid who was a decent singer. But nobody treated him like he was famous—until he spent several weeks on *Idol*. The TV show attracted tens of millions of viewers each week and received lots of coverage in the media.

Farnsworth looks into the screen of an early television receiver while he adjusts the dials. The circular disk at the right is the speaker.

"It feels like I'm a totally new person," he said. "I'm walking around as the same person I always was, but I could go in a store the week before I was on TV, and nobody would talk to me or say 'Hi, John' and know my name. The week after, they were like, 'Oh my God! I voted for you—I love the show!'"

▲ *American Idol contestant John Stevens performs at a concert in Los Angeles, California, on August 3, 2005.*

Not all of the feedback was so positive. On one episode, a popular contestant was voted off when many music industry experts thought that Stevens should have been the one to go. As a result, *USA Today* ran an article about Stevens with the headline: "Could this guy kill 'American Idol'?"

Ultimately, half of the twelve *American Idol* finalists were voted off before Stevens, meaning that he finished sixth in a contest that originally began with seventy thousand people. He received a flattering compliment from the most critical judge, Simon Cowell: "One of the reasons you are doing so well in this competition," Cowell told Stevens, "is that you are sixteen and you've taken every bullet thrown at you like a man."[6]

After the show, Stevens participated in a three-month tour with the top ten finalists. Put all together and despite the criticism that hurtled his way, Stevens said *American Idol* was "the best experience of my life."[7]

It was an experience made possible by the vision of Philo T. Farnsworth.

FARNSWORTH AND THE FUSOR

CHAPTER

5

The Farnsworths spent much of their time in the 1940s at a farmhouse in Maine. Phil had purchased the land and rebuilt the farmhouse into a cozy, comfortable home. He set up a laboratory, too. As he faced the pressures of developing television, and the disappointment of watching time tick away on his most important patents, he became depressed. Farnsworth turned to alcohol, and he drank so much that Pem once threatened to leave him. Eventually he got medical help and was able to regain his health. Through it all, the Maine farmhouse was a welcoming place where he could relax, think, and work.

One day in the fall of 1947, Farnsworth was on the phone with George Everson when the operator interrupted their conversation. A fire that had started at a lumber yard six miles away from the Farnsworth home was now headed his way. The flames would reach his property within twenty minutes. The Farnsworth family escaped with little time to spare.

Two days later, Phil and Pem returned to take a look at what—if anything— was left of their home. Everything was gone: The house. The lab. All of it. Smoking in its place were piles of charred ashes and melted metal and glass.

The Farnsworths lost not only their home, but thousands of dollars. The fire happened only days before Phil and Pem were to meet with an insurance agent and buy large cover- age for the property. Instead, they received only twenty thousand dollars—just a fraction of the Maine home's actual value.

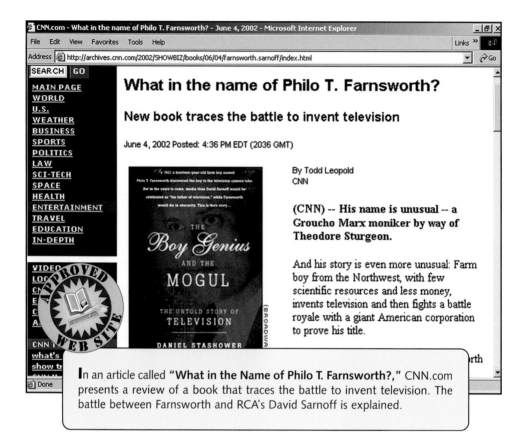

CNN.com - What in the name of Philo T. Farnsworth? - June 4, 2002 - Microsoft Internet Explorer

File   Edit   View   Favorites   Tools   Help   Links »

Address http://archives.cnn.com/2002/SHOWBIZ/books/06/04/farnsworth.sarnoff/index.html   Go

SEARCH GO

MAIN PAGE
WORLD
U.S.
WEATHER
BUSINESS
SPORTS
POLITICS
LAW
SCI-TECH
SPACE
HEALTH
ENTERTAINMENT
TRAVEL
EDUCATION
IN-DEPTH

VIDEO
LOO
CN
E
C
A

CNN
what's
show b

Done

What in the name of Philo T. Farnsworth?

New book traces the battle to invent television

June 4, 2002 Posted: 4:36 PM EDT (2036 GMT)

By Todd Leopold
CNN

(CNN) -- His name is unusual -- a Groucho Marx moniker by way of Theodore Sturgeon.

And his story is even more unusual: Farm boy from the Northwest, with few scientific resources and less money, invents television and then fights a battle royale with a giant American corporation to prove his title.

In an article called **"What in the Name of Philo T. Farnsworth?,"** CNN.com presents a review of a book that traces the battle to invent television. The battle between Farnsworth and RCA's David Sarnoff is explained.

⊖ FOCUSED ON THE COMPANY

The Farnsworths moved to Boston for the winter—which they had planned to do anyhow. Farnsworth, who had distanced himself from the day-to-day operations of his company, started to learn about what was going on. The news was not good: The Farnsworth Television & Radio Corporation was in bad shape. The public demand for television sets was huge—which should have been a good thing—but the Farnsworth company was having a difficult time getting parts from suppliers fast enough and in high enough quantities. Some of the parts were available only from RCA, and rumor had it that Sarnoff was using his influence to prevent Farnsworth from getting them.

So demand was up, manufacturing was behind, and Farnsworth could do nothing about it. He could only watch.

Worse, the company owed about $3 million to banks, and it did not have the cash. Farnsworth spent the next couple of years trying to reenergize the company. He brought in new researchers and started new projects, which made some money but not enough. Within less than two years, it was clear the company had to be sold. Offers came in

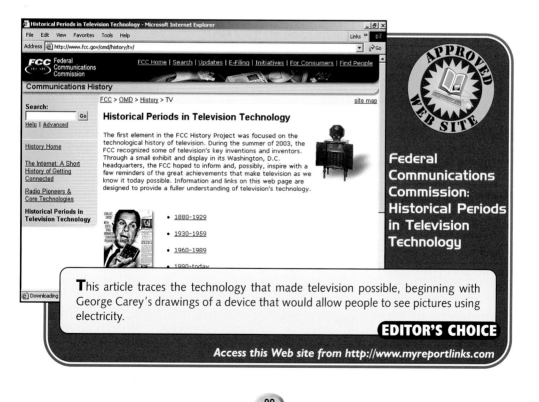

This article traces the technology that made television possible, beginning with George Carey's drawings of a device that would allow people to see pictures using electricity.

EDITOR'S CHOICE

Access this Web site from http://www.myreportlinks.com

from General Electric (GE), RCA, and a company called International Telephone and Telegraph Corporation, or ITT. It was ITT that won. At $1.4 million, the deal was a great one for ITT. Farnsworth's company was actually worth much more. But ITT executives did not want to be in the television business; they wanted Farnsworth as an employee.

Meanwhile, the rights to Farnsworth's patents that had not yet expired were sold to RCA, GE, and Zenith for $3 million. The price was a steal—the patents would certainly generate much more in profits. But it allowed the Farnsworth company to take care of those looming debts.

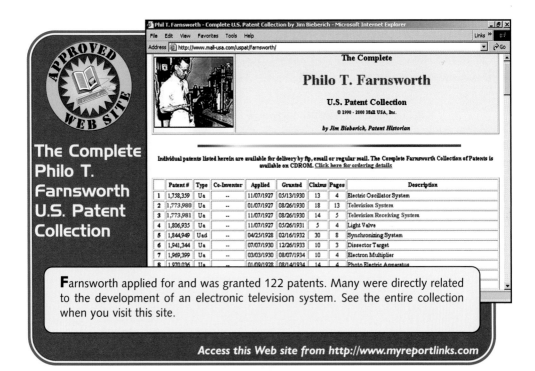

The Complete Philo T. Farnsworth U.S. Patent Collection

Farnsworth applied for and was granted 122 patents. Many were directly related to the development of an electronic television system. See the entire collection when you visit this site.

Access this Web site from http://www.myreportlinks.com

⇒ New Projects

Within months of the sale of his company to ITT and his patents to his competitors, Farnsworth was out of the day-to-day television business. He spent his workdays as an ITT employee developing technology that was used in air-traffic control equipment, submarines, telescopes, radar, the electron microscope, and early versions of the fax machine. Farnsworth's inventive mind also helped create the first infant incubator for babies born prematurely.

In his mind, he had moved on years earlier. During his years in Maine, Farnsworth spent a lot of time dreaming about the wonders he could accomplish with electrons. His most fanciful dream involved a process called nuclear fusion. Farnsworth envisioned using fusion, or the joining of two atoms, to create massive amounts of power very cheaply. Fusion already existed: The sun, and every other star in the universe, is a big ball of fusion. In the sun, atoms continually join together and, in the process, create great explosions of hot energy. That is why on Earth, 93 million miles (150 million kilometers) away from the sun, we can feel the heat of its rays.

Stars are not man-made, of course. They occur naturally in nature. Plus, the sun is not exactly safe. It is so hot that its rays can burn your skin and even lead to skin cancer. And if it were possible to ride a spaceship toward the sun, the heat would vaporize your ship into nothing long before you reached your destination.

Farnsworth, though, knew he could build a machine that created fusion, and he believed he could do it in a way that would be both safe and useful. Scientists had already made use of the opposite kind of nuclear science: fission, or the splitting of one atom into two. As with fusion, fission gave off massive amounts of energy. But unlike fusion, fission released harmful radiation. Fusion combined hydrogen and released helium, a safe gas. Fission had already been used to build

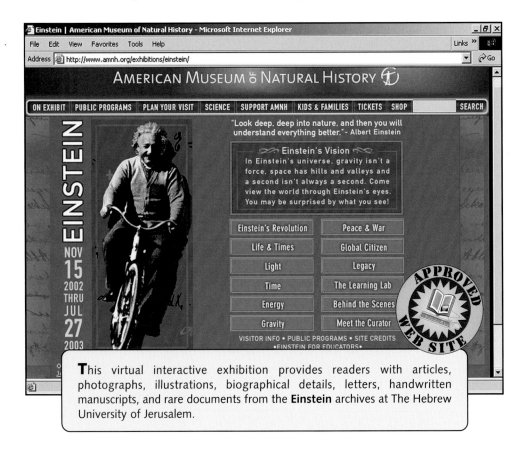

This virtual interactive exhibition provides readers with articles, photographs, illustrations, biographical details, letters, handwritten manuscripts, and rare documents from the **Einstein** archives at The Hebrew University of Jerusalem.

atomic bombs that resulted in explosions that were many stories high and caused widespread destruction wherever they were detonated.

Perhaps the most famous scientist who helped explain nuclear energy was Albert Einstein. Born in Germany in 1879, Einstein came to the United States fifty-four years later. He is generally regarded as one of the most brilliant people ever. Farnsworth had long idolized Einstein. He also knew that Einstein was one of the few people who could understand his vision for fusion.

⇒ MEETING EINSTEIN

One day in the summer of 1948, Phil and Pem visited their friend Frank Reiber in New York. Phil saw that Reiber had a painting of Einstein hanging on his wall. It turned out that Reiber knew Einstein, who lived in nearby New Jersey.

"You know, I'd love to talk to Einstein someday about some of these ideas I've been thinking about," Farnsworth said. Reiber told Farnsworth he oughtn't wait for "someday." Why not do it now? "Let me see if I can get Einstein on the phone for you."

Reiber went into another room to use the phone. He soon came back and told Farnsworth that Einstein was on the line. It turned out that Einstein knew of Farnsworth and was interested in his work. "He'd be delighted to talk to you," Reiber said.

Elma "Pem" Farnsworth greatly aided her husband in his endeavors and business ventures while he was alive, and fought to preserve his legacy after he had died. This photograph, taken in 1999, is of Pem displaying Farnsworth's portrait, journal, and a statute of him.

Farnsworth and Einstein talked privately for about an hour. Farnsworth learned that Einstein had envisioned similar uses for fusion. Einstein encouraged Farnsworth to continue his work.[1]

⇒ PURSUING FUSION

Farnsworth was thrilled. Einstein—one of his scientific heroes—knew him and believed in his work! Farnsworth carried that enthusiasm with him, even as his television patents and company were snatched up by larger, richer organizations.

While working on other projects for ITT during the early 1950s, Farnsworth spent his free time working on fusion. First, Farnsworth had to perfect the mathematical formulas that would one day guide him as he built a fusion machine. Farnsworth spent many evenings at home doing math on a large mechanical calculator. Called a MonroeMatic, this calculator looked and worked similarly to a typewriter. (Nowadays, Farnsworth could have used a computer to solve within hours the same math problems that took days on the MonroeMatic.)

As Farnsworth used his mathematical results to help plan his fusion machine on paper, he began to worry. He knew fusion could be incredibly powerful—and if used the wrong way, incredibly dangerous. Fusion could be used to make weapons that caused mass destruction. The inventor had an uneasy feeling about this. He wanted to create a machine that would generate safe and cheap energy for lighting cities, fueling automobiles, or even powering a ship through space. But he knew that wicked, destructive minds could take his technology and use it to create murderous weapons. Visions of a laser strong enough to burn a hole through the moon haunted Farnsworth's mind.

Worth the Risk

Eventually, Farnsworth grew more comfortable with making controlled fusion a reality. Two factors helped: First, Einstein had encouraged him to do it. Einstein knew the risks of fusion, too, but he also understood the potential benefits. Farnsworth trusted his fellow scientist's instincts.

Second, Farnsworth realized that atomic power had already been unleashed on the world. In the wake of World War II, the United States and other countries had used fission to develop and explode nuclear bombs. Nuclear weapons had already caused huge controversy. The United States and the Soviet Union were engaged in the Cold War, which was not an actual war but rather a race in which each country was trying to outdo the other in a variety of areas—nuclear weapons included.

Nuclear science was already a dominant force in the world. Why, Farnsworth figured, should I not create a positive use for it?[2]

⊜ Building the Fusor

Though Farnsworth envisioned fusion as a way to harness inexpensive power, building a machine to do it would not be cheap or easy. By the time Farnsworth was ready to begin building his machine, it was 1959. Phil and Pem's family now included two adult sons, Philo, Jr., and Russell, and a ten-year-old boy named Kent. They had little

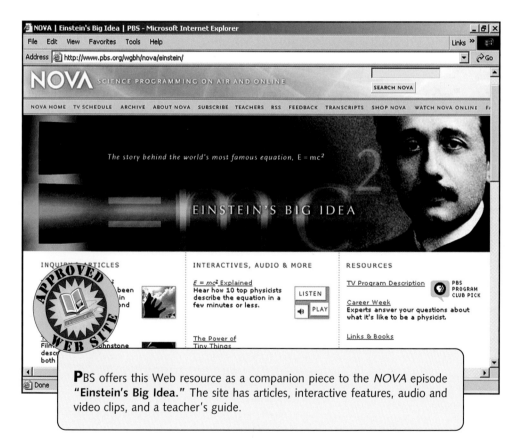

PBS offers this Web resource as a companion piece to the *NOVA* episode **"Einstein's Big Idea."** The site has articles, interactive features, audio and video clips, and a teacher's guide.

extra money, so they took out loans. Farnsworth started buying the materials he required—largely a collection of copper tubes and tanks—and set up a laboratory in a spare bedroom at home. He worked on the fusion machine each night. A few evenings every week, one of his ITT colleagues, Gene Marks, came over to help.

Originally, Farnsworth's bosses at ITT showed little interest in giving him money and time on the job to research fusion. After Farnsworth started working on the project at home and they realized he was serious, they reconsidered. Eventually, Farnsworth was given a limited budget to pursue fusion as part of his ITT work.

⊜Testing the Fusor

In October 1960, Farnsworth was ready to test his first fusion machine. Called the Fusor, the contraption was made mostly of glass and metal jars and tubes. Using a hydrogen-related gas, the Fusor was designed to create fusion in the center. If it worked, the Fusor would create a miniature star underneath the glass. That star would give off neutrons, or energy.

Farnsworth powered his Fusor, connected it to a vacuum pump to suck out the air, and released hydrogen atoms inside. A device called a Geiger counter, which detects neutrons, started clicking. This meant energy was being produced. The Fusor seemed to be working. Just to be sure, Farnsworth made some adjustments and retested the Fusor a few days later. The Geiger counter clicked again. The Fusor worked!

During the next few years, Farnsworth tested and retested the Fusor, improving it and building bigger, more powerful models. His bosses at ITT took notice. While they still were not nearly as excited as Farnsworth was over the prospects of nuclear fusion, they wanted to make sure he had highly skilled help. In 1964, a young scientist named Robert Hirsch joined Farnsworth on the fusion project. Along with their small staff, Farnsworth and Hirsch kept developing the Fusor. Eventually their models of the

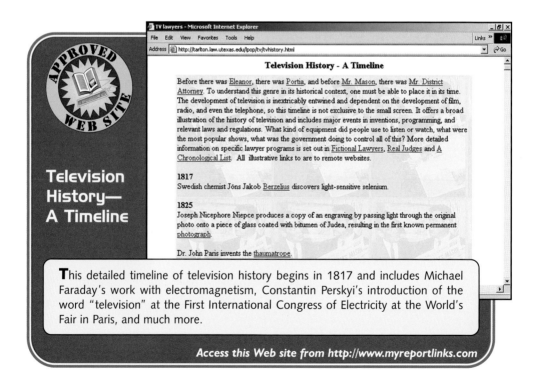

Television History—A Timeline

This detailed timeline of television history begins in 1817 and includes Michael Faraday's work with electromagnetism, Constantin Perskyi's introduction of the word "television" at the First International Congress of Electricity at the World's Fair in Paris, and much more.

Access this Web site from http://www.myreportlinks.com

machine grew big and powerful enough that the other workers were sometimes startled by the Fusor's powerful clicking, clacking, and sparking.

Farnsworth, however, never seemed to feel as if he got enough support from his bosses at ITT. One day, when Farnsworth and Hirsch were demonstrating the Fusor for guests, someone asked Farnsworth to explain a detail. An ITT executive who was also in the room had Hirsch give the explanation instead. Farnsworth was hurt. For him, this was the final blip in a long string of frustrations. He quietly exited the room and had Pem pick him up outside.[3]

RETIREMENT

Farnsworth retired from ITT in 1966, at age sixty. The Fusor was patented by ITT in the late 1960s, and Hirsch kept working on the technology. Eventually, however, the project stopped. Hirsch demonstrated the Fusor for United States government officials and asked them to provide money to fund further research. They decided against it, and so the Fusor project ran out of money.

Other scientists have tried to develop technology that uses controlled fusion as an energy source, but none have had great success. By most accounts, the scientist who best understood the concept was Farnsworth. But it seemed as though he was forced away from it. Maybe someday

A Geiger counter is an instrument used to measure the level of radiation in an object or area.

WARNING
PREVENT CORROSION
REMOVE ALL BATTERIES
WHEN NOT IN USE

another scientific genius will be able to pick up Farnsworth's work and, like Einstein, understand what Farnsworth was thinking. Then, if that scientist can develop fusion using twenty-first century technology, perhaps Farnsworth's vision of a fusion-powered world will become a reality.

FARNSWORTH'S LEGACY

CHAPTER 6

Philo Farnsworth invented television, but he did not particularly like it. As he watched television grow in popularity, he was not impressed with what he saw. Farnsworth thought that television was a huge time waster. Both children and adults spent hours every day watching shows of all kinds. They could spend those hours doing something active with their minds or their bodies. They could be reading or playing. Or, like Farnsworth did as a child, they could be building and inventing.

Farnsworth's youngest son, Kent, once said, "I suppose you could say that he felt he had created kind of a monster, a way for people to waste a lot of their lives. . . . Throughout my childhood his reaction to television was, 'There's nothing on it worthwhile, and we're not going to watch it in this household, and I don't want it in your intellectual diet.'"[1]

Farnsworth was so turned off by television's poor effects that it was barely used in his own home.

At one point, he had eight of them in the house, but none worked. One day when he was a boy, Kent came home from school crying. None of the kids believed that his dad had invented television. The reason? Kent was the only one among them who did not watch it at home. Farnsworth gave in and hooked up a television for Kent to watch.[2]

→ MYSTERY GUEST

For most of his adult life, Farnsworth was not recognized as the inventor of television. David Sarnoff's massive publicity efforts had buried Farnsworth deep in people's memories. Sarnoff was the boss of NBC, a network people watched nearly every night. They associated him with the beginnings of television. Farnsworth preferred to keep quiet and stay private. He did not talk much about himself, and so people did not think much about him.

Farnsworth appeared live on national television one time. In

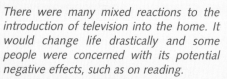

There were many mixed reactions to the introduction of television into the home. It would change life drastically and some people were concerned with its potential negative effects, such as on reading.

1957, he was a guest on a CBS show called *I've Got a Secret.* The audience was clued in to his achievement while a panel of celebrities had to guess what he had done.

As the mystery guest, Farnsworth was given the name "Dr. X." This threw off the celebrities' guesses. They thought he was a medical doctor.

The actress Jayne Meadows asked, "Does what you do cause pain?"

Farnsworth answered, "Sometimes it does, yes."

When Garry Moore, the host, finally revealed who "Dr. X" was, the comic Henry Morgan asked Farnsworth if he was sorry he had invented television. Farnsworth said no, he was proud of it. At

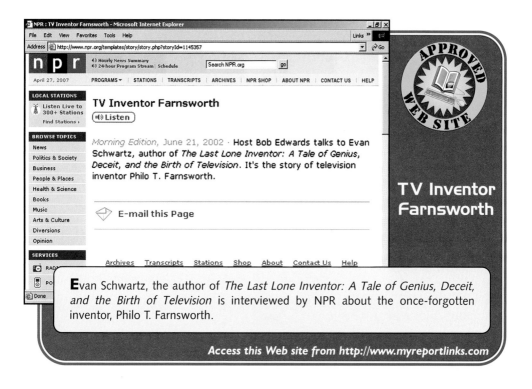

Evan Schwartz, the author of *The Last Lone Inventor: A Tale of Genius, Deceit, and the Birth of Television* is interviewed by NPR about the once-forgotten inventor, Philo T. Farnsworth.

Access this Web site from http://www.myreportlinks.com

the end, Moore thanked Farnsworth: "We'd all be out of work if it weren't for you."[3]

→ MAN ON THE MOON

Farnsworth had originally hoped television would provide a service to mankind. He wanted his invention to deliver important news quickly. He had hoped it would help people get important information instantly. Radio, of course, did this, too. But Farnsworth knew that a television picture would have incredible impact on people.

Farnsworth was right. For as much time as people spent watching Hollywood-created shows, they also got the chance to witness historical events. One of those happened on July 20, 1969. The *Apollo 11* spacecraft was flying to the moon. When astronauts Neil Armstrong and Buzz Aldrin stepped out of their *Apollo 11* spacecraft, they would become the first humans ever to set foot on the moon.

At this point in history, the United States was deep in a race against the Soviet Union to develop a strong space program. This lunar landing would be a major victory for America. And most Americans were watching, thanks to Farnsworth's invention. He had given them a front-row seat to history.

Phil and Pem sat in front of their television and watched history unfold. The astronauts were using a small version of Farnsworth's Image Dissector to show the world what they saw. After the spacecraft landed, Armstrong emerged. He planted his foot onto the moon's surface and said, "That's one small step for man, one giant leap for mankind."

It was also a giant leap into the heart and mind of Philo Farnsworth. He had long suffered mixed feelings about his invention of television. "He thought he'd maybe wasted his time because of the programming," Pem told in an interview years later. "But then when we saw the first man on the moon, he just changed his mind."[4]

Watching Armstrong step onto the moon and into history, Farnsworth turned to his wife. "Pem," he said, "this has made it all worthwhile."[5]

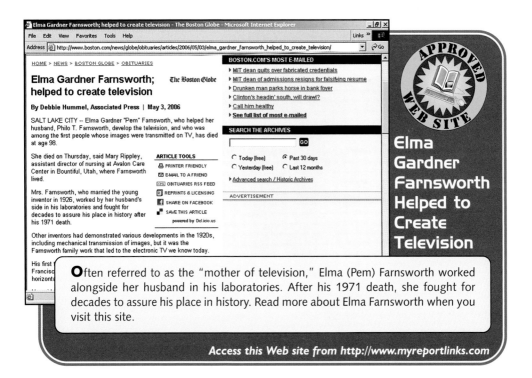

Often referred to as the "mother of television," Elma (Pem) Farnsworth worked alongside her husband in his laboratories. After his 1971 death, she fought for decades to assure his place in history. Read more about Elma Farnsworth when you visit this site.

Access this Web site from http://www.myreportlinks.com

⊜AN EARLY DEATH

Farnsworth grew sicker in the later years of his life. He died on March 11, 1971, after a bout with pneumonia. Farnsworth was sixty-four years old.

Pem, heartbroken, spent the next few years focusing on her family and church. But by the mid-1970s, she was ready to do something her husband never had: She was determined to fight for Philo Farnsworth's place in television history. Pem spoke openly about her husband's work.

She gave interviews, talked to politicians, and wrote a biography called *Distant Vision.*

Slowly, during the two decades that followed Farnsworth's death, he started getting recognition. A statue of him was placed in the United

◀ *In his later years, Philo T. Farnsworth made peace with what his invention had come to mean to the world.*

States Capitol. His face appeared on a postage stamp. He was inducted into the National Inventors Hall of Fame. Journalists started writing in-depth books about Farnsworth and his struggles against David Sarnoff. Hollywood writers wrote scripts for plays and movies about Farnsworth's life. In 1999, *Time* magazine named Farnworth one of the twentieth century's great scientists.[6]

Pem Farnsworth, who died in 2006 at age ninety-eight, stood by her husband's side throughout his life and after. He was the genius behind television, and she was his support. Farnsworth often told people, "My wife and I started this TV."[7]

Pem often visited schools to share her husband's story with children. She always delivered a simple message: "Anything is possible if you just try hard enough."[8] Nothing proves that better than the life of Philo Farnsworth. Sitting on a plow in Idaho at age fourteen, he dreamed the ideas that led to the invention of television. Within six years, he started making that vision a reality. He dedicated all of his energy to making television work, and it did. By the end of Farnsworth's life, the entire world was watching.

ACTIVITIES AND TELEVISION EXPERIMENTS

ACTIVITY #1

MAKE AN ELECTROMAGNET[1]

Philo Farnsworth taught himself a lot about magnetism and electricity at a very young age. He learned that electric current creates a magnetic field. Appliances from washing machines to computers to televisions use these electromagnetic fields. Here, you will create and test one:

MATERIALS:

- **a steel nail, three inches or longer**
- **three feet or more of copper wire, with thin insulation**
- **masking or duct tape**
- **D battery**
- **paper clips or iron shavings**

A burst of iron shavings has been attracted to this magnet. If you use iron shavings (also called iron filings) for Activity 1, be sure to keep in mind that they can be sharp.

Step 1: Wrap your copper wire around the nail in neat, tight spirals. The wraps should touch one another like coils on a compressed spring, but they should not overlap. Leave eight to ten inches of wire hanging off each side of the nail.

Step 2: If you have a lot of extra wire hanging off the nail, cut it so that both sides are eight to ten inches long. Remove about an inch of insulation from each end.

Step 3: Use the tape to connect one end of the wire to the positive end (pole) of the battery, and the other side of the wire to the battery's negative pole.

Step 4: When both ends of the wire are connected to the battery, you have an electromagnet. Use the nail to attract paper clips or iron shavings.

Points of caution: Be safe and be clean! When connected, your battery may become hot. Make sure your electromagnet is far away from wall outlets and other open sources of electricity. And be cautious with iron shavings—they are very messy and can be sharp.

⊜ THINGS TO TRY:

The electricity flowing from the battery through the wires aligns all the molecules in your nail in the same direction. When this happens, the nail becomes magnetized.

- **How much can you pick up? The stronger your electromagnet, the more**

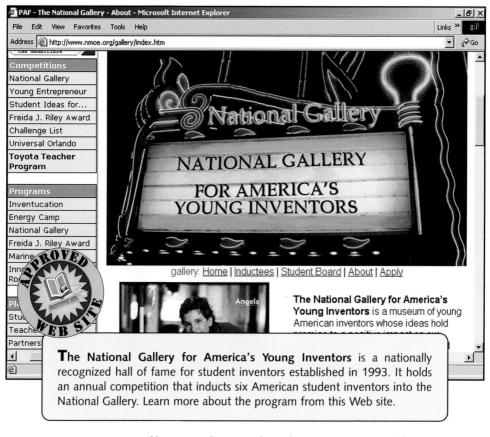

Address http://www.nmoe.org/gallery/index.htm

Competitions
National Gallery
Young Entrepreneur
Student Ideas for...
Freida J. Riley Award
Challenge List
Universal Orlando
Toyota Teacher Program

Programs
Inventucation
Energy Camp
National Gallery
Freida J. Riley Award
Marine
Inn
Ro

Pl
Stu
Teache
Partners

gallery: Home | Inductees | Student Board | About | Apply

Angels

The National Gallery for America's Young Inventors is a museum of young American inventors whose ideas hold

The National Gallery for America's Young Inventors is a nationally recognized hall of fame for student inventors established in 1993. It holds an annual competition that inducts six American student inventors into the National Gallery. Learn more about the program from this Web site.

paper clips or iron shavings your nail will attract.

- To strengthen your electromagnet, wrap a second layer of wire on top of the original coils. Be careful again to wrap the wires tightly and in the same direction, not overlapping.

- Disconnect one end of the wire. The paper clips or iron shavings should fall off. Your electromagnet works only when the electricity flows through it. Otherwise, it's not a magnet—just a nail wrapped in wire!

Activity #2

Put Your TV in "Focus"[2]

A picture can be broken apart and put back together again. Philo Farnsworth's Image Dissector did this electronically. You can accomplish a similar task using the lens of a magnifying glass.

⇒ Materials:

- **magnifying glass**
- **white plain paper**
- **a television**

Step 1: Turn on your television and turn off all the lights in the room.

Step 2: Stand approximately ten feet away from your television. Hold the paper in one hand and the magnifying glass in the other. Lift the magnifying glass until it is in line with the television screen. Hold the paper behind the magnifying glass so that the light from the television shines onto it.

Step 3: Experiment a bit. Change the distance between the magnifying glass and the paper. Move closer and farther away from the television.

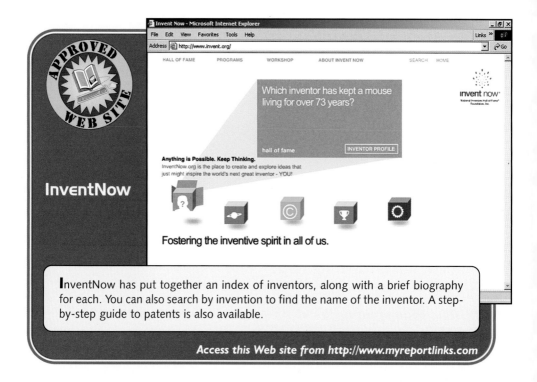

Invent Now - Microsoft Internet Explorer

File   Edit   View   Favorites   Tools   Help

Address http://www.invent.org/

HALL OF FAME   PROGRAMS   WORKSHOP   ABOUT INVENT NOW   SEARCH   HOME

Which inventor has kept a mouse living for over 73 years?

invent now
National Inventors Hall of Fame
Foundation, Inc.

hall of fame   INVENTOR PROFILE

Anything is Possible. Keep Thinking.
InventNow.org is the place to create and explore ideas that just might inspire the world's next great inventor - YOU!

Fostering the inventive spirit in all of us.

InventNow

InventNow has put together an index of inventors, along with a brief biography for each. You can also search by invention to find the name of the inventor. A step-by-step guide to patents is also available.

Access this Web site from http://www.myreportlinks.com

⊛QUESTIONS:

A lens collects and organizes light. Your television screen is a collection of millions of points of light that form a picture. When those lights shine on your lens, the lens focuses them in one direction.

- **What is different about the image on the paper compared to the picture on the television screen?**

   You will notice that the image is flipped. The magnifying lens turns it upside down and shows it backward.

- **How does changing the distance between the paper and the magnifying glass affect the image?**

This should help focus the image. Any camera works the same: You need to adjust the lens until the image looks crisp and clear. Because a magnifying glass is not as advanced as a camera lens, you may not get a perfect picture. But the idea of adjusting it until you come close is the same.

Report Links

The Internet sites described below can be accessed at http://www.myreportlinks.com

▶**Philo Farnsworth**
Editor's Choice *Time* magazine provides a look at the life and career of Philo Farnsworth.

▶**Farnovision**
Editor's Choice This Web site is dedicated to Philo Farnsworth and his invention of the television.

▶**Inventor Philo Taylor Farnsworth (1906–1971)**
Editor's Choice A *San Francisco Chronicle* article from 1928 discussing Farnsworth's inventions.

▶**Farnsworth's Image Dissector**
Editor's Choice IEEE History Center at Rutgers University has an article on the image dissector.

▶**Federal Communications Commission: Historical Periods in Television Technology**
Editor's Choice The FCC has an article outlining the historical eras in television technology.

▶**Library of American Broadcasting**
Editor's Choice This site follows the history of broadcasting.

▶**Baird Television**
A history of television, with a focus on the work of John Logie Baird.

▶**"Big Dream Small Screen"**
This PBS site provides a program transcript of the episode "Big Dream Small Screen."

▶**The Birth of Television**
Good overview of the invention of television.

▶**The Complete Philo T. Farnsworth U.S. Patent Collection**
A complete list of Farnsworth's patents.

▶**Early Television Foundation**
Historical information, photos, flyers, and vintage posters about television.

▶**Einstein**
American Museum of Natural History presents this online look at Einstein's life and work.

▶**"Einstein's Big Idea"**
View this online article about Einstein and his genius.

▶**Elma Farnsworth Passes at Ninety-Eight**
The Academy of Television Arts & Sciences pays tribute to the Farnsworths.

▶**Elma Gardner Farnsworth Helped to Create Television**
This article highlights the life of Elma Farnsworth.

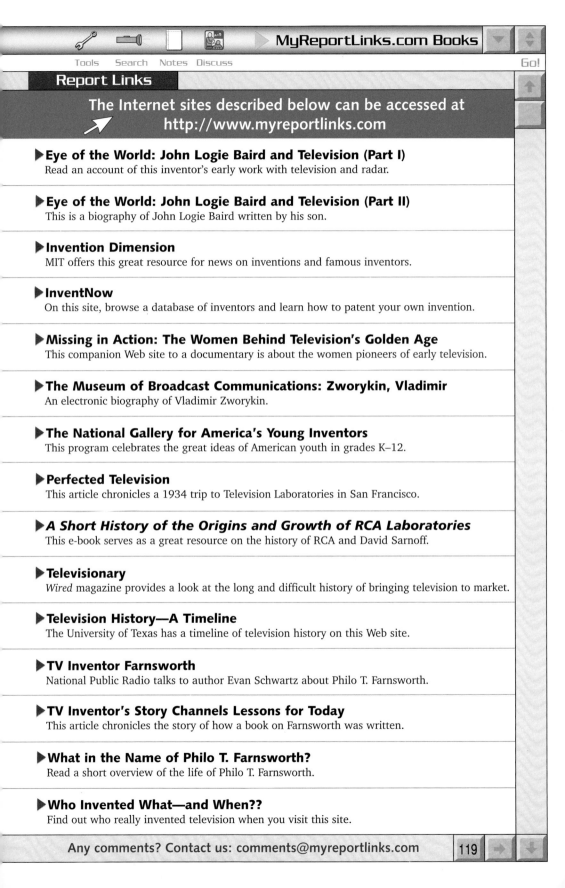
Report Links

The Internet sites described below can be accessed at http://www.myreportlinks.com

▶ **Eye of the World: John Logie Baird and Television (Part I)**
Read an account of this inventor's early work with television and radar.

▶ **Eye of the World: John Logie Baird and Television (Part II)**
This is a biography of John Logie Baird written by his son.

▶ **Invention Dimension**
MIT offers this great resource for news on inventions and famous inventors.

▶ **InventNow**
On this site, browse a database of inventors and learn how to patent your own invention.

▶ **Missing in Action: The Women Behind Television's Golden Age**
This companion Web site to a documentary is about the women pioneers of early television.

▶ **The Museum of Broadcast Communications: Zworykin, Vladimir**
An electronic biography of Vladimir Zworykin.

▶ **The National Gallery for America's Young Inventors**
This program celebrates the great ideas of American youth in grades K–12.

▶ **Perfected Television**
This article chronicles a 1934 trip to Television Laboratories in San Francisco.

▶ *A Short History of the Origins and Growth of RCA Laboratories*
This e-book serves as a great resource on the history of RCA and David Sarnoff.

▶ **Televisionary**
Wired magazine provides a look at the long and difficult history of bringing television to market.

▶ **Television History—A Timeline**
The University of Texas has a timeline of television history on this Web site.

▶ **TV Inventor Farnsworth**
National Public Radio talks to author Evan Schwartz about Philo T. Farnsworth.

▶ **TV Inventor's Story Channels Lessons for Today**
This article chronicles the story of how a book on Farnsworth was written.

▶ **What in the Name of Philo T. Farnsworth?**
Read a short overview of the life of Philo T. Farnsworth.

▶ **Who Invented What—and When??**
Find out who really invented television when you visit this site.

anode—The terminal by which electric current enters a cell.

atoms—The small unit of matter; it contains protons, neutrons, and electrons.

attorney—A lawyer.

cathode—The terminal by which electric current leaves a cell.

contraption—Another word for a gadget or simple machine.

electrons—The negative particles in an atom.

fission—The process of splitting the nucleus of an atom.

frequency—A way of labeling airwaves. Each radio and television station in an area broadcasts at a different frequency so that one station's signal does not overlap others.

fusion—The process of joining the nuclei of atoms.

harrow—A type of plow with sharp spikes or discs, that is used for smoothing out and turning over soil.

magnetism—The science that deals with magnets and why objects are attracted to one another.

negotiation—The process of trying to come to an agreement or make a deal.

neutrons—Particles in an atom that have neither a positive nor a negative charge; they make up the nucleus.

patent—A legal document that names the creator of an invention. The owner of a patent is granted exclusive rights to sell the invention.

protons—The positive particles in an atom.

radiotrician—An old term for a person who is expert at building radios and transmitters and doing other types of electrical wiring for radios.

receiving tube—A tube that converts radio waves into signals that can be received in a radio or television.

resolution—A way of measuring the crispness of a picture on a screen.

royalties—A payment made to an inventor for each item sold under his or her patent.

shares—A way of measuring the amount of money a person invests in a company. The more shares owned, the more money the person has invested.

stock market—A place where shares of a company are bought and sold.

transmit—To send out a signal over radio waves from one place to another.

vacuum—A space with no gas, air, or other matter.

weathercaster—A person who gives the weather report, usually on the radio or television.

Chapter 1. "There You Have Electronic Television"

1. Elma G. Farnsworth, *Distant Vision* (Salt Lake City: Pemberly Kent Publishers, Inc., 1990), p. 90.
2. Ibid.
3. Ibid., p. 91.
4. Ibid.

Chapter 2. How the Dream Began

1. Paul Schatzkin, *The Boy Who Invented Television* (Brutonsville, Md.: Teamcom Books, 2002), p. 10.
2. Evan I. Schwartz, *The Last Lone Inventor* (New York: HarperCollins, 2002), p. 10.
3. Ibid.
4. Ibid.
5. Ibid. pp. 26–27.
6. Schatzkin, p. 21.
7. Schwartz, pp. 53–54.
8. Elma G. Farnsworth, *Distant Vision* (Salt Lake City: Pemberly Kent Publishers, Inc., 1990), p. 4.

Chapter 3. The Dream and the Realities of Business

1. Evan I. Schwartz, *The Last Lone Inventor* (New York: HarperCollins, 2002), p. 124.
2. Ibid., pp. 135–136.
3. Paul Schatzkin, "An Eerie Electronic Hue," *The Farnsworth Chronicles,* 2002, <http://www.farnovision.com/chronicles/tfc-part03.html> (March 29, 2007).
4. Elma G. Farnsworth, *Distant Vision* (Salt Lake City: Pemberly Kent Publishers, Inc., 1990), p. 112.
5. Sparkletack, "Philo T. Farnsworth," *The San Francisco History Podcast,* December 2, 2005, <http://www.sparkletack.com/2005/12/02/philo-t-farnsworth/> (March 29, 2007).
6. Ibid.
7. Schwartz, pp. 177–182.
8. Ibid., pp. 86–88; quote from p. 187.
9. Ibid., pp. 200–201.
10. Farnsworth, p. 156.

11. Schwartz, p. 220.

12. Ibid., pp. 223–232; Farnsworth, pp. 178–181.

13. Schwartz, pp. 238–239.

14. Ibid., pp. 266–269.

15. Ibid., pp. 259–261.

Chapter 4. Life After the Arrival of Television

1. Mary Bellis, "The Invention of Television," *About: Inventors, 2007,* <http://inventors.about .com/od/tstartinventions/a/Television_Time_3.htm> (March 29, 2007).

2. Public Information Office, "50th Anniversary of 'Wonderful World of Color' TV," *U.S. Census Bureau,* March 11, 2004, <http://www.census.gov/Press-Release/www/releases/archives/facts_for_features/0 01702.html> (March 29, 2007).

3. Paul R. La Monica, "Super Prices for Super Bowl Ads," *CNNMoney.com,* January 3, 2007, <http://money.cnn.com/2007/01/03/news/funny/ superbowl_ads/index.htm> (March 29, 2007).

4. Kansas State University Information Technology, "History of Cable TV: The Early Days," *k-state,* 2006, <http://www.k-state.edu/infotech /cable/history.html> (March 29, 2007).

5. Michael J. Fox, *Lucky Man* (New York: Hyperion, 2002), pp. 124–129.

6. Author interview with John Stevens, January 2005.

7. Ibid.

Chapter 5. Farnsworth and the Fusor

1. Paul Schatzkin, *The Boy Who Invented Television* (Brutonsville, Md.: Teamcom Books, 2002), pp. 207–208.

2. Ibid. pp. 217–219.

3. Ibid. pp. 232–236.

Chapter 6. Farnsworth's Legacy

1. Mary Bellis, "Philo Farnsworth," *About: Inventors, 2007,* <http://inventors.about.com/library /inventors/blfarnsworth.htm> (March 29, 2007).

2. Evan I. Schwartz, *The Last Lone Inventor* (New York: HarperCollins, 2002), p. 291.

3. Ibid., pp. 291–292.

4. Charles Osgood, "Confusion over the real inventor of the television." *CBS News—Sunday Morning,* July 30, 2006.

5. Elma G. Farnsworth, *Distant Vision* (Salt Lake City: Pemberly Kent Publishers, Inc., 1990), pp. 327–328.

6. Neil Postman, "Scientists & Thinkers: Philo Farnsworth," *The Time 100,* December 8, 1998, <http://www.time.com/time/time100/scientist/profile/Farnsworth.html> (March 29, 2007).

7. Debbie Hummel, "Elma Farnsworth, widow of television pioneer, dies at 98," Associated Press, April 29, 2006; Sarah A. Meisch, "Mother of TV, Pem Farnsworth, dies in Utah at 98," *Fort Wayne Journal-Gazette* (Indiana), April 28, 2006.

8. Marianne Costantinou, "Pem Farnsworth—helped invent TV," *San Francisco Chronicle,* May 9, 2006.

Activities and Television Experiments

1. Experiment drawn from others posted at <http://www.scienceob.com> and <http://www.kidscanmakeit.com>.

2. "Light Action! Amazing Experiments for Children," *Optics & Photonics* News, December 1993, <http://www.opticsforkids.org/resources/KS_3.pdf> (May 29, 2007).

Casanellas, Antonio. *Great Discoveries and Inventions That Improved Our Daily Lives.* Milwaukee: Gareth Stevens, 2000.

Davies, Eryl, and Alison Porter, eds. *How Things Work.* New York: Barnes and Noble Books, 2003.

Hasday, Judy L. Albert Einstein: *The Giant of 20th Century Science.* Berkeley Heights, N.J.: Enslow Publishers, 2004.

Lackmann, Ron. *The Encyclopedia of 20th Century American Television.* New York: Checkmark Books, 2003.

Mattern, Joanne. *Television: Window to the World.* New York: PowerKids Press, 2003.

Niz, Ellen Sturm. *Philo Farnsworth and the Television.* Mankato, Minn.: Capstone Press, 2007.

Nobleman, Marc Tyler. *Television.* Mankato, Minn.: Capstone Press, 2004.

Richter, Joanne. *Inventing the Television.* New York: Crabtree Publishers, 2006.

Roberts, Russell. *Philo T. Farnsworth: The Life of Television's Forgotten Inventor.* Hockessin, Del.: Mitchell Lane Publishers, Inc., 2002.

Robinson, James. *Inventions.* Boston: Houghton Mifflin Company, 2006.